D1714458

*Our 20 Year Journey
as Missionaries to Scotland*

ECL Publications

The cover photograph is of the Eilean Donan Castle, one of the most recognized castles in Scotland and a Scottish icon. The photograph of the castle was taken by photographer George Hiles. His photograph is available on Unsplash.com.

Dedication Page

I would like to dedicate this book to a group of people who made this all possible.

First, to my precious wife, Denise, who has been beside me on this journey every step of the way. Without her, none of this would be possible, including the writing of this book. She has sacrificed greatly to see ministries be successful by giving her time, using her talents, and being my greatest supporter. She boarded three small children on a plane to Scotland and made a home for us.

To my college roommate, David Lee, who encouraged me over a year ago to write a book and didn't stop bugging me until I did it. He has been a true friend from the day we met, and I appreciate all of his help with this book.

To my parents, Phil and Carol Williams, who mailed out countless prayer letters, took care of our finances, and allowed us to live for months at a time in their home. Every missionary needs a support group like I had in my parents.

And last but not least, our three children: Anna, Ben, and Jared who were key members of our missionary team. It was a group effort, and they were a part of everything we did. They made the journey fun and gave us memories that will last a lifetime.

Table of Contents

Introduction

We quit and give up too easily.

I'm saddened by the number of Christians who quit and give up after one little thing goes wrong in their lives. In reality, God has blessed them over and over, but they fail to see His hand in their lives. So when something goes wrong, they are done. You never see them in church anymore. They become angry and bitter at God and just quit.

There was a stretch in Scotland when we had several missionary families come to the country. There had to be twenty or so families, probably more. But almost all of them returned to the States within a year. I thought, "How sad, Scotland desperately needs missionaries and these families all leave."

Perhaps they had unrealistic expectations, or things weren't working out for them. Whatever the reason, they packed up their belongings and left. I couldn't help but think of all the money that was wasted from churches supporting these families while they were on deputation and while they were on the mission field.

We don't understand God.

We don't understand how He works. We don't understand a whole lot about Him even though we have been in church for years. Things are not always going to go smoothly for us. We are going to face challenges. There will be disappointments. We will experience failure. The storms of life came to both the wise man and the foolish man in Matthew 7:24-27. Just because we are saved it doesn't mean that we aren't going to face storms in our life.

The Bible is filled with illustrations of great opposition towards believers. Ask Moses, Gideon, King David, Daniel, the Apostle Paul, or our Lord and Saviour Jesus Christ about opposition. We need to keep the faith. We need to plow through difficulties. We need to trust God when everything looks hopeless. We can make it.

How do we respond to God when we hear the word cancer from our doctor?

How do we make it when we are told that we just lost a loved one?

How will things go when we find out that we are going to lose our job?

We all face challenging times.

Challenging times began the day we started deputation. They continued the day we landed at Glasgow Airport in Scotland. They were there when we had our first church service. They never ended for the next twenty years.

No matter what comes your way, continue to trust God, and He will see you through. Don't quit on God and never give up. The same God who was there for Moses will be there for you.

I trust this book will be an encouragement to everyone who reads it no matter where you are in your life right now. Join us for our twenty-year journey to Scotland and back. It was full of challenges, but great times as well. Memories were made that will be with us for the rest of our lives. We are so thankful that God took us on this incredible journey to Scotland.

Barry Williams

Chapter 1
Without a Doubt

My Gideon Fleece

Judges 6:36-40 *"And Gideon said unto God, If thou wilt save Israel by mine hand, as thou hast said,*

Behold, I will put a fleece of wool in the floor; and if the dew be on the fleece only, and it be dry upon all the earth beside, then shall I know that thou wilt save Israel by mine hand, as thou hast said.

And it was so: for he rose up early on the morrow, and thrust the fleece together, and wringed the dew out of the fleece, a bowl full of water.

And Gideon said unto God, Let not thine anger be hot against me, and I will speak but this once: let me prove, I pray thee, but this once with the fleece; let it now be dry only upon the fleece, and upon all the ground let there be dew.

And God did so that night: for it was dry upon the fleece only, and there was dew on all the ground."

Gideon is told that he is going to save Israel from the Midianites. In Judges 6:16, God tells Gideon that He will be with him and that Gideon will smite the Midianites as one man. Gideon is told everything that he needs to know, yet he has doubts about all of this. Gideon gives God excuses in verse 15, and then he wants a sign from God. We refer to the next part of this story as 'putting out the fleece.'

People often criticize Gideon for putting out the fleece, but I don't. Sometimes, it's hard to figure out what God wants us to do.

There were times in my life when I had no clue what God wanted, and sometimes it took forever to try and figure it out. Then, even after figuring it out, there have been times when I still wasn't sure, and I had my doubts. Let's be honest, we don't want to do something outside of the will of God or something that God doesn't want us to do.

When it came to making the decision to go to Scotland... that was a huge step for me. To take your wife and three little kids to another country without having much of a clue as to what we would be doing once we got there, that was a big step. Even to begin the process of raising funds two years earlier was a big step. I remember praying to God and telling Him that if He really wanted me to do this He had to make Himself clearer to me.

I told God I was going to call one of the well-known churches of that day, Landmark Baptist in Cincinnati, and speak to Dr. Harold Rawlings and ask him for a meeting. If God wanted me to go to Scotland then He needed to get me a meeting at Landmark. Much to my surprise, Dr. Harold was in... he took my call... he told me how much he loved Scotland... then he asked me to come and present my ministry the next Wednesday.

After I hung up, I just stared at the phone.

To be honest, I think we all have doubts at times. I don't think there is anything wrong with that. Joshua surely had doubts, and we see that Gideon had doubts.

What is wrong is when we figure out what God wants us to do,

and we don't do it... then that, my friend, is a problem.

God's Provision

As a missionary, there have been countless times when God has miraculously taken care of us. The time I remember the most was early on in our deputation journey. We were in this small country church somewhere in Ohio, I can't recall where we were. The next day both car payments were due and something else big was due, it could have been the rent. All I remember is I needed about $1000, and I had less than $100 in our checking account.

It was a beautiful summer day. I was sitting on the steps of the church before the service and in my mind I was thinking, "God, how are you going to pull this one off?" I began to doubt if God really wanted us to go to Scotland. All sorts of negative thoughts ran through my head. There was no way this small church could come close to giving us $100 let alone $1000.

We had a good service, and they took a love offering for us. We loaded up the kids and headed home, dejected. I was running through my head how I could come up with the money that I needed for the next day. I gave Denise the check that the church had given us and asked her to tell me how much it was. Denise said, "Barry, you won't believe this, but this check is for $1200."

That was a defining moment in my life.

I knew from that moment on that God wanted us in Scotland, and He was going to take care of us each step of the way. God didn't need a church of 1,000 people to provide the money I needed to cover my bills that were due the next day. God didn't even need a church.

Somehow, someway, God always takes care of us.

Trust and Obey

God has a plan for us. He has a path for us to go down. The question is... will we trust Him? It sounds easier than what it really is. But in the ministry and on the mission field, you must have a high level of trust in God. You could call Proverbs 3:5-7 my life verses.

"Trust in the LORD with all thine heart; and lean not unto thine own understanding. In all thy ways acknowledge him, and he shall direct thy paths. Be not wise in thine own eyes: fear the LORD, and depart from evil." Proverbs 3:5-7

These are familiar verses and ones I've really had to hang on to at times in my life. We face trials, situations, difficult decisions, and problems that we just don't have any easy answers to.

God has moved us at various times. The biggest was taking three small children, along with some of our belongings, and loading them on a plane to be missionaries in Scotland. It's quite daunting to get on an airplane with three little kids and go to a new country and culture. There are so many unknown factors. Doubts fly through your head...

Am I doing the right thing?

Is this what God really wants?

Where are we going to live?

How am I going to start a church where I don't know anyone?

Where is this church going to be located?

What cultural difficulties are we going to run into?

Did we raise enough money to stay here?

What about schooling for the children?

God took us down a path that at times seemed impossible to go down, but in the end, God was completely faithful. We just had to trust Him.

If you are doing exactly what God wants you to do, God will equip you with everything you need for the task in front of you. Don't ever forget that. What you have to be careful about is that you are doing exactly what God wants you to do. If God isn't in what you are trying to accomplish, you will be better off trying to paddle a canoe up Niagara Falls. Instead of having doors open for you... you will have them slammed in your face.

God opens doors that seem impossible to open, and He will equip you with everything you need. Do you need a car? No problem. God knows that you are going to need a car, and God will provide one. The second house we looked at in Scotland was the one we rented. The guy who owned the house was moving to California. While signing papers for the house, he wanted to know if we would be interested in buying his car because he hadn't been able to sell it. In less than two hours, we had a beautiful house and a car.

All the while God kept telling us to just trust Him. Did God take care of everything for us? Absolutely. It wasn't a smooth ride every step of the way. There were some serious bumps in the road. We faced a lot of obstacles. We had our Jericho moments. There were battles to be won, and there were times when it was hard to trust God, but we kept putting our trust in Him.

God worked out every detail as He promised, and He directed our paths. God took us places we thought we would never go. He brought people into our lives that were an incredible blessing to our family. We simply had to put our complete trust in God. It all comes back to trust. Are you going to trust God with what you are facing?

Chapter 2
Friendly Fire

Homer Smith

I've been fortunate to have some amazing people help me in my life. They have shared their wisdom, insight, and knowledge with me. I have learned so much from them that I treasure those times we sat down and talked.

When I was just starting out on deputation, I was in a mission's conference up in Michigan that featured an incredible man as the main speaker for the conference. The church had a mission house and that is where this guest speaker and I stayed that week. Each night we would stay up really late and talk. He was a man of incredible wisdom, and he taught me so many things during those late-night talks.

God brought this man into my life at the right time and place. It was like God gave me a personal tutor for the week. One of the things I remember most is that he told me people would discourage me from going to Scotland. I was kinda stunned by that statement. Why would anyone discourage me from going to that country? But I can't even begin to tell you how right he was.

I had all sorts of people tell me not to go to Scotland, including heads of mission boards... one at the very next conference I was at!

I often wonder if I would've ever ended up in Scotland without this man coming into my life. Here's to Homer Smith. He will be one of the first men I look for when I get to heaven. May each of us have an impact on others like this man had on me.

Facing Opposition

When we were raising money to go to Scotland, there were many people that tried to discourage us from going there. I was in a missions conference with a well-known head of a mission board, and he pulled me aside after one of the services. He looked at me like I was crazy and asked, "Why in the world would you ever go to Scotland?" He told me that no American missionary had been successful there. He said it was a graveyard for missionaries, and it would be a waste of time and God's money for me to go there. I was told I would be more useful in a country that was more receptive to the gospel. He wanted my pastor's name and the name of my mission board. He was going to prevent me from going to Scotland.

I've never asked my pastor if that guy ever called him, but it gave me a great dislike for people who try to play God and pretend to know God's will for your life. I think if you asked the people of Scotland, for the most part, they are happy that I stepped into their country. I know I'm glad our family went there.

There will always be people who are going to try and discourage you from doing what God wants you to do, even men who run mission boards and other important people. From my own experience, simply make sure you are doing what God wants you to do and then just go out and do it. It doesn't matter what others say or what their opinions are.

God told Joshua three times in Joshua Chapter 1 to be strong and of good courage. God was preparing Joshua for a great task. I imagine one of the things God was preparing him for included the 'friendly fire' of well-meaning people. Just follow what God has placed in your heart no matter what others say.

Critics and Doubters

I've had many Gideon moments in my life when God has asked me to do something that made no sense. One of the biggest was the church building that God provided for us in Glenburn, Scotland.

Our church had just been asked to leave the community centre we were meeting in. We looked all over for a church building and found an old Baptist Union Church that had closed its doors. We had looked at some rough church buildings that needed major work done to them, but this building was in near perfect condition compared to the others.

We signed a contract to lease the building even though we had just a handful of people at the time. In fact, the building had a hefty price tag for such a small number of people, yet I knew deep down that we were going to get this building somehow... some way.

It was during this time that I got some 'friendly fire' from the Baptist brethren asking me how I was going to pay for the building. I heard comments like, "Well, this is a nice building and all but how are you going to pay for it?" What they failed to realize is that I wasn't the one who was going to have to pay for it.

God brought us to the building, and from my past experiences, I knew deep down that God was going to bring the money in. Without making this story too long, God provided the money for a down payment, and the church paid off the loan in less than 20 years.

When God brings a Gideon moment into your life, you are going to have to trust Him. God will make the situation look impossible, but if He is in it, God will come through in the end. Expect some 'friendly fire' as well. There will always be doubters giving you negative comments, just remain true and faithful to God.

Chapter 3
Traveling

Long Days

Early on when we began raising support to go to Scotland, there were some Sundays when the day began at 5:00 a.m. Sometimes the churches couldn't afford a hotel for us to stay in on a Saturday night, and we certainly didn't have the money for one, so we would need to leave as early as 5:00 a.m. on a Sunday morning to get to where we were going that day.

We had a Subaru station wagon at the time, and we would put the back seats down which would make a perfect bed for our children to sleep while I drove for about 4-5 hours to the church we were going to. The kids were little at the time, and the three of them fit perfectly in the back. On Saturday night, Denise and I would pack up the car and make a space for their beds knowing it was going to be an early morning. I would carry the children down from their beds, settle them in under their blankets, and off we would go.

Usually, by 8:00 a.m., everyone would be waking up so we would stop at a McDonald's to get breakfast. We would take the kids into the bathroom and get them dressed for church. Then we would put the seats up in the car and drive for another hour or so.

Our children would be in a different church every Sunday morning, Sunday night, and sometimes every Wednesday night. This means that they didn't know their teachers for Sunday School or Junior Church nor any of the kids in their classes, and they did this every week.

After each morning church service, our children would stand with us at our display table talking to people until the last person left. They would help us pack up our display and load it into the car. Afterward, we would all go out to eat with the pastor or another church family. Once lunch was over, we would travel another 3-4 hours to another church for a Sunday evening service and do it all over again.

Depending on how much time we had, we would sometimes stop at a McDonald's in between church services to let the kids play in the play area. Then on the road again to the evening service where once again they wouldn't know any of their teachers or children in their classes.

After the Sunday evening service, we would once again go out to eat with the pastor for an evening meal. After the meal, we would put the seats back down so the kids could sleep on the long journey home. There were nights when it was 1:00 in the morning before we got home. We would end the day like we started it by carrying the kids back up to their beds. The next morning, even after a long Sunday, they were up and ready to go to school.

The reason I'm telling you all of this is because I've heard comments that people have made about missionaries and their children. Comments that reveal a total lack of understanding of what these kids have to go through every week. I've been in churches and heard comments from church people that they would never support that missionary family because the kids weren't well behaved, or the children were running around. I knew of one church that determined who they supported based on the children's behavior.

Keep this in mind when the next missionary family comes to your church. Hopefully, this will give you a little insight into what those children do every week.

Caring People

The month of March is a big month for missions. Many churches have their missions conferences in the spring. When we were raising funds to go to Scotland, there were times when we would have a meeting almost every day in March due to all of the church conferences that were taking place.

I remember one stretch where I preached 21 straight days in a row. We would jump from one missions conference to the next. It was busy, but we really did enjoy it. We met so many wonderful people on our journey. We had the opportunity to meet great missionary families, and the church people were always so sweet. There were incredible church dinners too where we had a lot of good meals.

As I look back on those days, I'm always so thankful for all of the people that took our family in. We stayed with incredible families that would do everything possible to make us feel at home. The ladies would be up early fixing our kids whatever they wanted for breakfast. Our kids were four, six, and eight when we started traveling, and for our children it was like being at grandma's house because everyone was so hospitable.

Families took our children sled riding, four wheeling, played games with them, and did so much to make it fun. The churches would take all of the missionary kids bowling or have other activities lined up.

When we go back to some of these churches, it's great to catch up with the people that our family stayed with all those years ago. We are forever grateful to everyone who did so much for us. Those who opened their homes to our family, cooked meals, spoiled us with gifts, and just made our family feel at home. You have given us a lot of precious memories.

We are thankful for so many people.

Those who sacrificed financially to keep our family on the mission field.

Those who prayed for us.

Those who wrote us letters or sent our children birthday cards.

Those who opened up their homes to us.

Those that prepared meals.

Those who set up for mission dinners.

Those who taught our children in their Sunday School class.

Those who took our kids to activities or played games with them.

Those who were the last to leave the church and shut off the lights.

There are so many people who have had a part in our journey.

A special thanks to all of you!

May each of us do something to make life a little bit easier for those missionaries who stop by your church.

The photo we had taken for our first prayer card - June 1996
The children were 4, 6, and 8 years old.

Chapter 4
Welcome to Scotland

Things Didn't Go As Planned

One of the first things you learn when you go to the mission field is that things probably won't turn out how you had them planned. We learned this lesson as soon as we stepped off the plane in Scotland.

We had everything organized and ready for our arrival. We made sure every detail was taken care of. We spent hours making sure everything was set. What could possibly go wrong?

We flew into Glasgow International Airport on June 15, 1998. After clearing customs, we soon realized that the person who was to pick us up never showed up. What was worse is that the airline lost all of our luggage, all we had were the clothes on our back.

In addition to all of that, the people who owned the house we rented had their plans change at the last second which delayed them from moving out of their house for another week.

This meant that we couldn't move into the house we rented when we arrived in Scotland. But not only did we rent their house, we also bought their car which meant that we couldn't get that for another week either.

So on our first day in Scotland, we had no one pick us up at the airport, the airline lost all of our luggage, we couldn't move into the house we rented, and we had no car.

Welcome to Scotland!

Thankfully, we were able to rent a car at the airport, and the house rental company was able to find another furnished house for us that we could rent for only one week.

But the house was in another city, a city we had never been to and one that we were not familiar with. We had no idea where a grocery store was in that town. We also needed to find sheets and blankets for the beds and everything else we needed, and we had no idea where to go to find all of these things.

So there we were, hungry and tired from the long flight and the time difference, driving around looking for stores to buy all the things we needed.

Though it was a long first day in Scotland, and absolutely nothing went according to plan, we finally got most everything we needed. We got the kids fed. We got the kids settled in that first night and finally got to sleep ourselves. It was a rough start to our lives in Scotland, but at least we made it.

And if you are wondering about our suitcases and luggage....

It all arrived two days later.

Welcome to Scotland!

Erskine

When our family arrived in Scotland, we needed to find a house to rent for one week until we could move into the original house we had rented. The rental company found a house for us to rent in the town of Erskine. Of course, we didn't know much about Erskine when we first moved there, but for the next twenty years, Erskine became a town that we visited quite frequently.

We would often shop in Erskine, and a branch of our bank was there. The town had a really nice golf course that we played on several occasions. There was an indoor swimming pool that we took the kids to, and we also found a few good places to eat. Many years later, my wife would work at the library in Erskine.

Through our stay in Erskine, we found an excellent eye doctor that ended up being our eye doctor the entire time we lived there. For a family where everyone wears glasses, this was an important find.

But without spending our first week in the town of Erskine, I doubt we would have ever spent any time at all in that little town. It's interesting how God drops you off in certain places for a short period of time that actually become an important part of your life.

Right after we were married, Denise and I spent only one year in the town of Wintersville, Ohio, but it was a year that changed our lives.

We taught in the Christian school there, and I coached all sorts of sports. The principal of the school was Randy Sells. He spoke at almost every chapel, and his messages had a massive impact on my life. Randy and his wife, Debbie, are still good friends of ours 35 years later. He is now a pastor in Wintersville, and his church has supported us as missionaries for 25 years.

Another couple from those early days in Wintersville are Lenny and Jayna Peeler. We enjoyed our time teaching with them both at Wintersville and later at the Carroll County Christian Academy. Lenny even got one of our beagle pups. Today, he is a pastor right across the Ohio River in West Virginia, and his church has also supported us for 25 years.

It is almost like a reunion when we go back to the churches in that area. We get to see some of the students that we taught as well as their parents. Again, we only spent one year in Wintersville, but the town and the people in that town had a great impact on our lives.

God doesn't make any mistakes.

He puts us in places sometimes that may not make much sense to us in the beginning, but there is always a reason.

We lived in Erskine for just one week, but in that one week it became an important town to us, one we probably would have never gone to if not for a change in plans.

We wonder at times why God has placed us where He has us. Instead of complaining, see the good where God has placed you. There is a reason, even though it might not make sense to you today.

Another Setback

Although Scotland is an English-speaking country, we still had some adjustments to make. Things are different in another country. But after three short months of living there, we were ready to start a church in a neighboring town not too far from our house in Johnstone.

Starting a church takes a lot of work. Fortunately, we had another missionary and some of his church members come and help us pass out fliers. We had been attending their church while we were getting settled in Scotland, and they were a tremendous help to us. They eventually sold us a church van so we could give people a ride to church. We still have fond memories of that missionary family and their church.

Denise and I spent hours upon hours passing out fliers to let people know we were starting a church. We, of course, didn't know anyone in the area. But as soon as the kids went out the door for school in the morning, we were out the door to pass out fliers and invite people to our church. We passed out fliers all day until the kids came home from school. It was long, hard work.

Then we had a setback.

While playing ball at the park with the neighbor kids, our son, Ben, slid into second base, and I heard a snap. He was hurt and couldn't get up so I picked him up and carried him to our house. It was a Saturday night and the emergency room would have been packed. Because of this, one of our neighbor ladies told us to wait until early Sunday morning to take our son to the hospital.

So early the next morning, I took Ben to the hospital, and sure enough, he had broken his leg.

Normally a broken leg wouldn't phase us at all. We had been in the ministry for almost 15 years at this point, and we had dealt with a lot. But it just seemed like it was one more thing to deal with coming to a new country.

For us, the timing couldn't have been worse.

We didn't need it, and yet God allowed it to happen.

I was reminded of the words that God gave Joshua... be strong and of good courage. God repeated this phrase to Joshua time and time again when he was taking over for Moses.

Though this broken leg knocked the wind out of our sails for a couple of weeks, eventually we were right back at it again.

We are going to have setbacks in life. They may come at a time when you really don't need them and yet... here they are. The important thing is to get back up on your feet again and keep moving forward.

Setbacks come.

They are part of life.

Sometimes they come at your breaking point when you don't think you can handle one more thing.

Be strong and of good courage. You will make it.

Chapter 5
Where to Go?

Paisley

When we were trying to figure out what city God wanted us to go to, it was a really tough decision. Scotland is filled with some beautiful cities and all of them needed a good gospel witness. We traveled all around on our survey trip looking at one beautiful town after another.

Fort William is a stunning city right on the water. Scotland's highest peak, Ben Nevis, is behind the city so you have the water in front of you and beautiful mountains behind you. It was about two and a half hours up the coast from Glasgow. Who in their right mind wouldn't want to go to that city?

Inverness is another beautiful city. It's right on the water as well, and in any direction you look there are majestic mountains all around. Inverness also provides the perfect spot to sit by the water and watch dolphins and seals swim by.

St. Andrews was by far our favorite city. This coastal town has beautiful beaches and nothing but golf courses all around you. Being a golf nut, who wouldn't want to live in the 'home of golf?' The town itself was just stunning with cobblestone streets and little shops. I could go on and on about the beautiful cities in Scotland.

But there was one city that we really didn't like and that was Paisley. We jokingly said, "Anywhere but Paisley, God."

And guess where we spent most of our ministry?

Paisley!

The humor of God. Maybe we should have said, "Anywhere but St. Andrews, God." But God always knows what He's doing.

We fit right into Paisley with its people and culture. Some of the greatest times of my life can be traced back to that town which, at first, we really didn't like. In fact, Paisley was our home for many years. It was the town where we started our first church and where my wife got an incredible job. Our youngest son went to college in Paisley and through our church, he met his wife and later married her at that same church. We lived in many places over the years, but in the end, we came back to Paisley to live.

Many times we look around and think we will be happy in this city or that city.

But the truth is you will only be happy where God wants you.

When I attended Liberty University, Dr. Falwell always used to tell us that there is no better place to be than in the center of God's will. As I grow older, I can only say how true that is. We try to knock doors down and run through God's stop signs to get to where we think we need to be only to come to the realization that God wasn't really in our decision-making at all.

Right now we live in Mansfield, Ohio. We had a lady say to us, "Why would you live in Mansfield? You lived in Scotland and could have chosen any place in the U.S. to live and you chose Mansfield?" She went on forever about how bad of a place Mansfield is to live. To be honest, I would've never chosen Mansfield either, but it's where God has us. God knows what He is doing.

Chapter 6
Starting a Church

Finding a Building

A church needs a place to meet, and in Scotland there were several buildings in each neighborhood known as community centres that provided a great place to start a church. A good majority of these community centres were owned by the government.

When we were looking for a building to rent for our first church in Paisley, we came across the Brediland Community Centre (the correct spelling in Scotland is 'centre' as opposed to the American spelling 'center') and decided to rent it for our church.

One stipulation on renting the building for church services was that we had to have a caretaker present when we were in the building. So not only did we need to pay to rent the building, but we had to pay the caretaker as well.

It took the council a while to find someone who was willing to be a caretaker for us since we met on Sundays. We were very fortunate to have someone who was willing to do that for us because we rented the building not only for an hour in the morning, but we rented it for the evening service as well which meant that the caretaker had to come in twice on Sundays.

So with a building rented and a caretaker in place, we were ready to start our first church in Scotland!

Brediland Community Centre
Cardell Road
Paisley Scotland

We originally began our church as Southside Baptist Church and later changed the name to Glenburn Baptist Church after moving from this location to the church located on Braehead Road.

Don't Quit

The Sunday morning for our first church service arrived. It was a beautiful morning and a great day to start a new church. We had passed out thousands upon thousands of fliers. We talked to people in the community. We prayed and fasted for this church. We did everything possible to make sure our first Sunday was going to be a great day. I remember putting our church sign out in front of the community centre that first morning and being anxious and excited.

But when it was time for church to begin, no one was there. *No one*. After all that hard work, no one showed up for our first service. We waited about ten minutes, but still no one came. I wasn't sure what to do next. This wasn't how our first service was supposed to go. We went ahead and sang some songs with our children, and I gave a lesson. Our first service ended up being just the five of us.

A million questions ran through my mind. Did I just pick up and haul my family over to Scotland for nothing? Was this a massive mistake? I can't even begin to describe what I went through that day, but deep down I knew that all of this wasn't a mistake. I knew I should be in Scotland.

The time came for the evening service. We had a bunch of children show up and one man, at least we had some people come. We had our church service and afterward I talked to the man for a while, but we never saw him again. I made sure all the children got home safely, and then we packed up the car and headed home.

It wasn't a glamorous start by any stretch of the imagination. But every week we would get everything planned for church, and every Sunday we would go to the community centre and have everything ready for both the morning and evening services.

We did all of this for the next two months even though no one came for our Sunday morning service. It was just the five of us. This brought a lot of questions into our minds.

Should we quit?

Should we give up?

Should we move and try to start in another area?

We had more questions than answers. The only saving grace was that people started coming to our evening service. It wasn't long until we had 10-15 people coming every week on a Sunday night, but on Sunday mornings we still had no one.

Then one Sunday night our regular people said that they were going to start coming on Sunday mornings, and sure enough, they did. Pretty soon we were having over 20 then 30 people show up every week for both services.

My main point is don't give up.

If you think deep in your heart that you are where you should be, and you are doing what God wants you to do… don't give up.

When you have no one come to your morning service for the first couple of months… don't give up.

When nothing is going how you thought it would go… don't give up.

It would have been so easy to quit. Even today, when I go back to Scotland and return to that beautiful church building that was purchased for those people, I sit back and thank God that He gave us the courage not to quit…. don't give up.

A Permanent Place to Meet

By the time May rolled around our church attendance at the Brediland Community Centre had become pretty consistent. We had also gained help from another missionary family who we met at a missions conference here in the States. They lived about an hour and a half away and helped with the services.

Everything was going well until one Sunday the caretaker told me that I was to set up a meeting with the government official who was responsible for renting out the community centres. So I called and made arrangements for a meeting.

At the meeting, we were told that they had decided not to allow us to rent the community centre any longer because they had changed some of their policies regarding these buildings. We also couldn't rent out any of the schools in the area because they too were managed by the government. They told us that we had until the end of August to find another place to hold our church services.

Now what?

We were a church without a building. After talking with the church people, we decided to look for anything we could meet in, but we were praying for a church building.

There were many empty church buildings and we looked into them, but most of the churches had extensive damage and others were in such terrible shape that it would have cost us thousands to fix them. We didn't have much money so we were limited by our finances.

Denise and I spent hours looking at church buildings only to have our hopes crushed time and time again. There just seemed to be nothing available.

We were passing out fliers one afternoon, and I started up a conversation with a man who was working outside at his house. We began talking, and I told him we were looking for a church building. He told me that his mom's church had closed down and the building was sitting empty. When I asked him where the church was located, he told me it was only a couple of minutes from the Brediland Community Centre where we were currently meeting for church.

I was so surprised. I'm sure I passed this church many times, and yet I never noticed it. How could I not notice a church building? He gave us a number to call and off Denise and I went to drive past the church.

The outside of the building looked incredible, but I must admit my first thought was, "I wonder how damaged it is on the inside?" We went ahead and set up a time to look at the building. I remember opening the auditorium doors and being surprised at how nice everything was. It was just perfect like God spared this building from vandals just for us. There was no damage. It was 'move-in ready.' It had a nursery, a kitchen, a gymnasium, and a good-sized auditorium with a baptismal.

It was perfect for us.

After having the church people come and look at the building, we signed papers to rent the property. The rent was a little bit higher than the community centre, but not by much.

We held our first service in the new church building on July 18, 1999. God knows our needs, and He always takes care of us. You can count on that principle. It doesn't matter where you are in life or what you are facing… God knows, and He will provide a way.

Glenburn Baptist Church
91 Braehead Road
Paisley Scotland

The top picture shows the main door and the auditorium part of the building. The lower picture is of the gym and kitchen area.

The auditorium at Glenburn Baptist Church
with the original wooden benches.

This is how the auditorium looked the day we rented the building from the Baptist Union. The walls were painted a dark turquoise color up front. We eventually painted the auditorium a more neutral color, replaced the wooden benches with cushioned, stackable chairs, and had a larger platform area built.

Our home, Glenburn Baptist Church manse (parsonage)

Chapter 7
Glenburn

Glenburn Baptist Church

In Scotland, our first church was located in an area called Glenburn which is a part of Paisley. It was there that we were able to purchase a beautiful church building, Glenburn Baptist Church.

The church had an auditorium that we managed to get 130 people in on one Sunday. The church had a lovely kitchen and a courtyard area that we used a lot, as well as a gymnasium which was used for church dinners and kids clubs. I always looked at this church building as a miraculous gift from God.

There were many missionaries in Scotland that didn't have their own church building. They met in community centres or schools and weren't given the opportunity to have their own building like we did. So I always tried to instill into the church people that we have to take the best possible care of this gift we were given. I'm not sure they always grasped this concept, but I always did my best to instill in them that we needed to take care of what God had so graciously given us.

I always liked the property at the church to be neatly mowed with beautiful grounds on the outside and always freshly painted and looking sharp on the inside. I never thought it was a good testimony for the church property to look like a rundown mess.

Proverbs 24:30-32 *"I went by the field of the slothful, and by the vineyard of the man void of understanding; And, lo, it was all grown over with thorns, and nettles had covered the face thereof, and the stone wall thereof was broken down. Then I saw, and considered it well: I looked upon it, and I received instruction."*

The Bible doesn't really tell us if there are two different men with two different properties here or if it is just talking about one person, but whatever the case this person, or persons, are described as slothful and void of understanding. For the sake of argument, let's say they are two different men.

They have been given something precious, a field and a vineyard, but what they did with their properties was basically nothing. The one was too lazy to work in the field that he was graciously given. The other perhaps didn't understand what a precious gift he had in the vineyard. Either way, they didn't take advantage of what was given to them.

We've all run across properties that look like Frank and Mike from *American Pickers* should go and visit them, but in a way, I always find those situations sad. We have been given so much by our God. It could be properties or talents and abilities.

What are we really doing with what our God has so graciously given us?

Do we have talents and abilities that He has given us that need to be cultivated?

Do we have relationships, or even our relationship with God, that we have allowed to become overgrown with weeds and nettles?

What does our field or vineyard really look like?

Have we become slothful or lack understanding in areas of our life that simply need to be cleaned up?

Molly

I met Molly when she started coming to our church in Scotland, Glenburn Baptist Church. Molly was one of the sweetest, most precious women that you could ever meet.

She was also one of the most influential people you could meet. She wasn't loud or boisterous, she just led by example. Every woman in our church desired to be like Molly. She was a shining example of what every woman should be.

Even into her 90's, Molly would walk to church every Sunday even though she lived over a mile from the church. She always insisted on walking instead of having someone pick her up. I would stand out on the sidewalk in front of the church and look up the street and watch until I could see her walking towards the church. Then I'd run up to meet her and walk with her the rest of the way to church until she got inside our church building.

Almost every Friday, after I had all my messages finished up for Sunday, I would go to Molly's and just sit and listen to her stories. She lived through Hitler's bombings of Glasgow and told me what life was like during that time. She couldn't understand why children got so much for Christmas today. In her day you got an apple, and one year for Christmas she got a stick, a stick from a tree. A different life from what children have today.

Molly was a member of a lawn bowling league. (This isn't ten-pin bowling like we have here in the States) I believe Molly was 91 when she made the finals in the singles competition for her bowling league. She was an intense competitor. I went to watch the final that year, and though she lost she was surrounded by more celebrations than the winner who was some 30 years younger.

Molly's bowling league would use our church gymnasium to bowl indoors during the winter months. Every Tuesday morning, I would go to the church to get the bowling mats out and have everything ready for Molly's group.

A couple of times a year our church would have an indoor bowling competition against Molly's bowling club. It was a fun afternoon of bowling, food, and fellowship. The winners were presented with a trophy that we affectionately named 'Molly's Cup.'

One year when our church people were bowling against the members of Molly's bowling league, I was pitted against Molly. She looked at me and said, "You will lose today." Trust me she had no mercy on the preacher! I have a picture of Molly and me from that day, and I will always treasure it.

Molly passed away at the age of 96.

She was a wonderful example to all and faithful to God's house right down to the very end.

Agnes

The first time I met Agnes she was walking her dog, Bruce, past the church at Glenburn. Actually, Bruce was walking Agnes! Bruce was a stout yellow Lab and a massive dog. Agnes was a little woman who was hanging on for dear life. When I saw Agnes, I stopped cutting the grass at the church and went over to talk to her.

Agnes told me that she and her daughter, Jane, had been members of the church before it closed down and that Jane was head of the Brownies in the area. I told her I'd love to have Brownies in the church and invited them to come for services Sunday morning. They came that Sunday and hardly ever missed a service for the next 17 years. Agnes and her daughter were key members in that church and a true godsend.

Agnes became like a mom to Denise and me and a Scottish grandmother to our children. She loved us like we were her own. We spent hours at her house talking, having tea, and sitting down at meals together. We loved listening to her stories about growing up in Paisley and working at the Brown & Polson factory on Falside Road.

Agnes had insight into people like I've never seen before. She could just read people. I spent hours talking to her about the church and church problems because of the insight that she had. What I liked most about Agnes was that she was always brutally honest with me. She wasn't afraid to say perhaps what everyone else was thinking. She didn't care if I was the preacher or not. She just spoke her mind.

Agnes was a hard worker in the church. Even into her 70's, she helped at all the kid's clubs, summer camps, Awana, the Ladies' ministries, and church dinners. You name it, Agnes was a part of it. She didn't slow down once she was retired.

Another thing that I appreciated in Agnes was that she always wanted what was best for the church. She never had an agenda. Her primary concern was for the church.

As she got older, she would line up some of the younger wives in the church and give them the 'what for,' telling them they needed to take better care of their husbands. If Agnes was getting after you… you'd better listen!

She showed many of the young ladies in the church how to sew, knit, cook, and do all sorts of things. She was a great teacher, and she always had time for you. She was never too busy to do something for others.

Agnes was well respected in the church. Everyone went to Agnes, young and old alike, for advice, a friendly chat, a helping hand, or an encouraging word. She was just that kind of a person.

Our churches need more people like Agnes in them.

Sadly, Agnes passed away in 2021. There will be a massive void in the church at Glenburn from the passing of this dear, sweet, wonderful lady.

Autistic Children's Ministry

The Glenburn church had a ministry to autistic children and their parents. I was always so proud of the people in our church that worked with this group. As you can imagine, it wasn't the easiest ministry they could've signed up for. Our church people were always so compassionate and kind not only to the children but to their parents as well.

Those families with autistic children had to fight with the government for everything they could get, most of the time losing. I heard the parents say more than once that no one cared for them, so when they were invited to our church on a Saturday they were met by church people who did care for them. Our church family not only donated their time but they donated supplies and funds to make Saturdays a lot of fun for the children and their families.

The church people helped the autistic families, but they also helped out in many other ministries as well making a difference in the lives of those who needed it the most. People are looking for someone to care about them and take an interest in them. People are looking for help, and shouldn't the church be the place where they find it?

The church should be a place of refuge and safety in the midst of a world of troubled storms. The world needs to see the compassion of Christ in Christians today instead of the condescending, judgmental Christians they meet in most churches.

Our churches need to take a look at their communities and determine where the greatest need is and make an impact on the lives of children and adults alike.

We need to make a difference.

Daycare

Statistics tell us that the average father spends about a minute a day with his children. *One minute.* What do you think our homes are going to look like, and how will our children turn out if a dad spends one minute a day with his children?

While in Scotland, our Glenburn church had a daycare for children. Our church didn't run the daycare, we just rented out our church facilities to people who ran it. The daycare opened at 7:00 in the morning and didn't close until 6:00 at night. There were many children that were dropped off when the daycare opened, and they didn't get picked up until 6:00 at night when it closed.

I always thought to myself, "Who is teaching these children? Who is giving them the necessary instructions needed to prepare them for life? Where are their parents, and what is so important that they have their children in daycare for almost 12 hours a day?"

Do you really want to give the responsibility of training your children to complete strangers?

Deuteronomy 6:7 *"And thou shalt teach them diligently unto thy children, and shalt talk of them when thou sittest in thine house, and when thou walkest by the way, and when thou liest down, and when thou risest up."*

God gives clear instructions to parents. It is their responsibility to teach their children about the things of God. We are not to pawn the responsibility off to others. We are not to expect the youth pastor in our churches to train our children to make up for our failure to obey God in this area. The teaching of your children is the responsibility of you, the parents.

What have we allowed to come into our lives that takes us away from this great God-given responsibility of ours?

I hear all the time, "We have bills to pay." Let's be honest -

We have chosen to live above our means rather than invest in our children and take care of this responsibility of ours.

We have chosen to have more things rather than take care of this responsibility of ours.

We have chosen to impress our friends with our big house and fancy toys rather than take care of this responsibility of ours.

We have made a conscious decision to allow other things to come above the training of our own children. We have sold out our children for things, and our children see this.

The older generation in Scotland was brutally honest in our church. They would ask younger families questions like, "Why do you need such a big house?" or "Do you really need that fancy car?"

It used to crack me up to hear them ask these questions, but they were always exactly right. They knew that in order to have all of these things the children in the home were going to be neglected.

Chapter 8
Holidays

Easter

We did many different things for Easter, but having a sunrise service wasn't one of them. I tried to have a sunrise service one year and was quickly told that no one would be there. We did eventually have an early service at 9:00 a.m. on Easter Sunday even though some still thought that time was way too early as well.

For many years we had a church dinner, and then when we began to have the 9:00 a.m. service we switched from a church dinner to an Easter breakfast. We had a couple of ladies in the church that cooked the breakfast pretty much by themselves. It was always incredible, and it definitely got more people to the early service. To this day, I'm not sure how they cranked so much food out of that kitchen, but they did. It was always a good, proper Scottish Breakfast.

Our church people always did a great job of getting visitors out for Easter. People generally come to church at Easter and Christmas, but you still have to ask them to come. Easter was always one of the best-attended services of the year as it is here in the States. With the early service, we normally didn't have an evening service. Most people spent the rest of the day with their families.

Easter in Scotland always meant that better weather was coming. Though we didn't get much snow, we did have a lot of rain in the winter with howling winds. Winters were miserable with it being so cold, dark, windy, and wet.

Easter gave everyone hope that better weather was coming.

The Fourth of July

The Fourth of July wasn't quite the same in Scotland. In fact, we never really got to celebrate this holiday very much. They didn't have fireworks, and if they did you would have to stay up until around midnight to see them because the sun doesn't go down until really late this time of year in Scotland. As the kids grew older and started working, the Fourth of July was just another day of the work week.

I always enjoyed British History because the nation is so much older than ours. In their schools they have a different take on our American Independence Day... they teach it as The Rebellion of 1776! It was so funny the first time I heard The Rebellion of 1776 because growing up in America you just never think of how others view the same historical event. To them, it was a rebellion against the king and the British throne.

I wonder sometimes how God views things compared to how we view them. Just our sin alone, which nailed God's Son to the cross, there is obviously a big difference in how we view our sin compared to how God views it.

What about some of the things that take place in our churches? It could be a disagreement or a church split. We have our take on it, but how does God view it? God has all the facts. He knows man's heart, his motives, and his urge for power. God knows who twists the story around to make themselves look good. God knows everything.

We view ourselves as good and correct, but what is God's take on the matter? We like to think our actions are justified, but what is God's take on the matter? I had an old preacher friend that used to say, "You better hope God lines up with you in these matters."

Christmas Songs

Christmas was always one of the most exciting times of the year in Scotland. The church family would come together to decorate the church on Sunday afternoon in between the morning and evening services. It was like the church was completely transformed by the time the evening service started. Everyone always did an exceptional job in making the church look so beautiful. It was just stunning, to be honest. It was like the church was built especially for Christmas. You almost wished you could leave the church decorated like that for the entire year.

Probably one of the things I miss most about Scotland are the Christmas songs. Many of the songs are sung with different words or a different tune than what we are used to here in America. They are beautiful arrangements, but completely different.

I can't remember all the details, but I was a guest speaker for a company's Christmas gathering the first year we were in Scotland. When I got to this place of business, I was informed that the person who was to lead the music couldn't make it so I was asked if I would lead the music. As most of you know, this isn't one of my top ten talents, and what really made it difficult was that I found out real quick that hardly any of the Christmas songs were sung the same way that I was used to!

I picked out about ten of my favorite songs and gave them to the piano player. When she began the introduction to the first song, "*Away in a Manger*"... I knew I was in trouble. I think only two or three of the songs we sang that day were the same. I explained the problem early on to the people, and we all laughed about it. They sang so beautifully that day. I just sat back and enjoyed all the different arrangements of the Christmas songs.

Christmas Eve

Early on in Scotland, we had our Christmas Eve service at 11:00 at night. It was a tradition with that group of church people so we kept their tradition. We sang Christmas songs, and I gave a Christmas message. The church was just beautiful, especially in the candlelight.

The service would last until midnight and then we would go down to the gym for a time of fellowship for another hour or so. We would have tea, coffee, and all sorts of Scottish baked goods. They made little mincemeat pies, and there was usually a yule log along with all sorts of cookies that we never saw here in the States. Everything we had to eat was amazing.

At that time we lived right beside the church and since it was 1:00 in the morning when we got home from the Christmas Eve Service, we just opened up presents with the kids. We were all up anyways so we just had Christmas a little bit earlier than everyone else. That became a tradition for our family for the remainder of the time we lived in Scotland, even after we moved the Christmas Eve service up to a more reasonable time of 8:00 p.m.

Needless to say, we had a few more people show up to the 8:00 p.m. service. The last couple of years in Scotland we had the young adults bring a concert, and we had all sorts of special music. The music was always incredible. It was just a great service and an opportunity to share the gospel with people who normally don't attend church.

Christmas Around the World

One of my favorite Christmas services in Scotland was what we called 'Christmas Around the World.'

At that time in our ministry, our church was a mixture of many different cultures. There had been a lack of professional people in Scotland so the government allowed people who were part of the British Empire to emigrate to the United Kingdom based on a point system. We had people from Zambia, Zimbabwe, Botswana, and South Africa who emigrated to Scotland based on this point system. Most of the ladies were nurses, and their husbands were engineers. They were just wonderful people, and we enjoyed so much having them be a part of the church.

With Great Britain being a part of the European Union at that time, we also had people from Greece in our church. Other countries like the Philippines were represented; and, of course, we had people from the States. I'm probably forgetting some countries, but we had a really neat mixture of cultures in our Glenburn church.

One year, we asked every country represented in our church to share their Christmas traditions. It was amazing to hear how each different culture celebrated Christmas. Many of the people sang Christmas songs in their native language.

It was just an incredible Christmas service and one that I will never forget.

Chapter 9
God's Will

Livingstone

One of the most difficult things for me to figure out is what God's will is for my life. I'm not sure why I struggle. It could be that I just don't want to make any mistakes. I don't ever want to be where God doesn't want me. There have been times in my life when it has taken me a little longer to figure out God's will than it probably should have. One of those times was while we were in Scotland.

A missionary in the town of Livingstone was going to return to the States, and he had no one to take over his work. At that particular time, there were two of us working in the church at Glenburn so it only seemed fitting that one of us should take his work. After praying about it, I agreed to move our family to the town of Livingstone on the other side of Scotland.

The problem was we couldn't get any housing. It didn't matter what house we looked at, God completely shut the door.

The first house we looked at we just loved, and it looked like God was going to make everything simple for us. We put in a higher bid than everyone else to make sure we would get the house, but the homeowners *took a lower bid.*

One evening we were driving around and saw a builder putting the finishing touches on a house. We stopped by and asked him if he had a buyer, and he told us he didn't have one. We thought for sure this was the house God had for us. It was out in the country in a really nice area. It was perfect.

The builder told us to come by his office around 10:00 the next morning to sign the papers. We thought, "Well, this is a done deal." In the morning we drove over to his office only to find out that *an hour earlier* someone came in and bought the house.

We saw another house on the internet that we really liked so we called the owners and asked if we could come over to see the house. It had just come on the market, and no one had looked at it yet so we were feeling pretty confident about this house. We loaded up the kids for the hour drive to Livingstone.

But when we got there the owners said, "We are so sorry a couple just bought our house." This couple was just out for a walk, and they saw that the house was for sale. They knocked on the door, went through the house, and *bought it on the spot*.

This is just the beginning. I could sit here and tell you story after story how God closed one door after another when it came to us getting a house - I told you I was a little slow.

I finally called my preacher and told him what was going on, and he simply reminded me that when God is in something... everything just falls into place. He said it was obvious to him that God wasn't in this move.

To make a long story short, another missionary took over that work.

Looking back, every time we've moved God has provided us a house almost immediately. It's always been the first or second house we have looked at. When God is in something He always has everything fall into place, and it is actually really simple.

If you have looked at 50 houses... God probably isn't in that move.

Doing What God Wants

Acts 9:6 *"And he trembling and astonished said, Lord, what wilt thou have me to do? And the Lord said unto him, Arise, and go into the city, and it shall be told thee what thou must do."*

I can't stress enough how important it is for you to be where God wants you. Not where everyone else wants you... but where God wants you. People will try and manipulate you to get you to where *they* think you should be. There are people who should have been on the mission field and they aren't, and there are others who were on the mission field that shouldn't have been on the mission field at all. Much of life has to do with people trying to manipulate you.

I'm not saying don't get advice from others before you make decisions, but find people that really don't have a bias one way or another in the advice they are giving you. Finding people without bias can be very hard at times. I went through a spell of about six months where it seemed I couldn't find one person that didn't have some sort of agenda in their advice to me.

You need to make sure God has the final say.

There were all sorts of people who tried to discourage Denise and me from going to the mission field. Important people. People who had a great influence on our life. But for me, it always comes down to - what does God want?

God doesn't always make His will clear at times, and it can be hard to figure out exactly what God wants. But if you are really seeking out His will, God will open and close doors as He sees fit. You might make mistakes along the way, but you will find your way. Just make sure you are following God's will for your life... not your will and not the will of others... but God's will.

Chapter 10
Our Second Church

Helensburgh

Ezekiel 22:29 *"The people of the land have used oppression, and exercised robbery, and have vexed the poor and needy: yea, they have oppressed the stranger wrongfully. And I sought for a man among them, that should make up the hedge, and stand in the gap before me for the land, that I should not destroy it: but I found none...."*

The second church that we started in Scotland was located in the town of Helensburgh. There was a naval base near the city so as you can imagine this town had all sorts of Navy families stationed in the area. We got to meet many of these families. Some of them came to our church or their children came to our children's clubs.

We originally met in a Scout Hall for church services, and then a short time later we moved to a community centre that was run by the Navy. They were very accommodating to us in Helensburgh because we had three families in the church that had military ties.

They were also willing to give us a break on our rent for the building if we ran youth clubs. Sunday afternoons we had probably 30 kids or better that came out for soccer. The community centre had real soccer goals which we would set up after the Sunday morning service.

We also ran Awana. Since the primary school wasn't far from the community centre, we held Awana right after school. We ended up having so many kids that we had to have Awana on two different afternoons.

Because the men were serving in the Navy, many of the fathers or husbands would be gone for months at a time. I always felt so sorry for the wives and children. The little children would be without their dads for extended periods of time and it would just break your heart. You could tell the children missed them a lot. They were always so excited when their dad's submarine returned to the base.

I know these military families had all sorts of needs. The wives and children needed so much help. Our churches need to step up in areas like this and make a difference in the lives of others. Doing little or nothing for others is not acceptable. I see so many churches that have absolutely no outreach at all. We have to do better than this. We have to do more than just come to church for a couple of hours and then go home.

What are the needs in your area? How can you make a difference in your neighborhood? What single mom really needs some help? What can you do to make someone's life a little bit easier? We need to make a difference. This world needs Jesus. How can we bring Jesus to them?

Churchhill Community Centre
Helensburgh Scotland

Helping the Next Generation

There was a couple that started coming to the Helensburgh church who were two of the most precious, sweetest people you could ever meet. Their last child had just moved out of the house so they were enjoying life as 'empty nesters.'

This couple got saved in their mid 40's. I went to their house every Tuesday night to disciple them. They were such a joy to teach. They both soaked everything up that I taught them. They were so excited about the Christian life and life in general, especially for this new phase of life they had in front of them.

This all changed very rapidly.

Sadly, one of their daughters, who had a little son, got hooked on heroin and became a heroin addict in a very short time. Their life became one horrific nightmare. To make a long story short, this couple had to adopt their little grandson, and instead of being empty nesters they now had a little boy to raise.

But in spite of all the heartache of watching their daughter destroy her life, they were excited for the opportunity to raise this little boy in a Christian home.

Let me tell you, there is a fatherless generation out there that needs you. God may not ask you to adopt a child, but you can make a difference in your community and in your church.

You can help a generation of children who have no one to teach them about the things of God. They have no one to teach them how to be a godly father or mother. You may still have children in your home or you may be empty nesters, but there is a generation out there that needs you and needs you now.

Chapter 11
The Farms

Tandlemuir

We lived in some incredible places in Scotland, probably my favorite were the two sheep farms we lived on.

The first one was called Tandlemuir Farm. It had a section of the house that was believed to be built in the late 1600s. Yes, you read that right... the 1600s. The living room in the house had a fireplace that you could throw an 8-foot log in. It was an unbelievable fireplace. What was fascinating about that house though wasn't the fireplace, but the walls and foundation of the house.

The outside walls were at least 3 feet thick. You could easily sit on the window sills to look out into the fields. There was also a little basement under the original part of the house. The foundation was built with massive rocks. I wondered how anyone could move them and place them where they did for the foundation of this house.

You may be wondering, why such thick walls and a foundation like that?

Storms.

Some of the winter gales in Scotland shook everything. I really can't describe the gales, but many times they were fierce. The damage sometimes was just astonishing. But the way that farmhouse was built it could handle pretty much any storm that came its way. It had a strong, solid foundation.

Storms are necessary in life. They are brought into our lives to teach us and to make us stronger. Storms give us more faith and make us more like Christ. Storms even give us confidence in knowing that we handled that storm that just shook our foundation…We made it.

The number of Christians that become bitter and angry with their God when one little thing goes wrong in their life shows us that there are a lot of Christians out there with little or no foundation whatsoever. They stop coming to church, and it isn't long until they are completely out of church. It's almost like they will only be faithful to God as long as everything is going smoothly for them. This isn't much of a faith at all.

Matthew 7:24-27 *"Therefore whosoever heareth these sayings of mine, and doeth them, I will liken him unto a wise man, which built his house upon a rock.*
And the rain descended, and the floods came, and the winds blew, and beat upon that house; and it fell not: for it was founded upon a rock.
And every one that heareth these sayings of mine, and doeth them not, shall be likened unto a foolish man, which built his house upon the sand;
And the rain descended, and the floods came, and the winds blew, and beat upon that house; and it fell: and great was the fall of it."

How solid is your foundation?

Is your foundation able to withstand the fiercest storms of life?

Can your foundation only handle a small wind?

Let's keep working on that foundation. Keep trusting God through the storms of life. Your storms are there for a purpose, understand that and keep growing and building on that foundation.

Stray Sheep

Tandlemuir Farm belonged to an older farmer and, to be honest, the farm needed some work. The fences were always down so the sheep would roam and go where they weren't meant to be. Often the farmer would ask us to help him find his sheep. So the boys and I would go out and walk the hillsides looking for stray sheep.

We found one sheep with its head stuck in a fence, and another time we found one wrapped around briars literally hanging about five feet above a stream. We were always finding sheep in places they shouldn't be and we would always wonder, "How in the world did that sheep end up there? What was that sheep thinking?" The one tangled up in briars dangling above the stream was a real mystery. We had no idea how she ended up there.

Often when I see people that I've not seen for 20 or 30 years, I wonder to myself, "How in the world did that person end up there?" People that were once on fire for the Lord are now in a place that is completely void of God and His love and protection. Like those sheep, they are in a place they shouldn't be.

We really need to keep our relationship with our God strong. I find it stunning how nonchalant we can be in our walk with God. Watching people fall by the wayside should make us strive to walk with our God in a greater way. We also need to take care of a fallen brother or sister in the Lord. They may need someone to listen to them, encourage them, or help them get untangled from the briars they have found themselves in. They don't need a condemning voice. They need a helping friend. They know they've messed up.

It also reminds me how much we need to pray for one another. The devil is good at destroying the lives of people.

Night Games

I always enjoyed having the youth group over to our house for night games. One of the games I loved the most was a game that was like hide-and-seek. In our version, you had the option of running back to 'base' for safety or you could keep on hiding until 'time' was called for the game to be over. You just didn't want to be the first one caught or the last one caught because those two individuals would be 'it' for the next round.

When I was a pastor here in the States, we had about 80 teens that would come to our house for night games. The kids would spend all night at our place. The boys would sleep outside in tents, and the girls would camp out in the house. We always had a pig roast the next day and invited the whole church out for a huge dinner. We had a bonfire, shot clay pigeons, played tackle football, and just had a great time.

But one of the neatest places to play night games was in Scotland on Tandlemuir Farm. We limited the area we played in to about seven acres so we didn't lose anyone.

There were so many places to hide. There were stone walls to hide behind and piles of fallen trees. There was a huge area that had 4 foot high ferns. I've never seen ferns that big. If you lay down under these ferns and stayed quiet no one would find you unless they stepped on you... which did happen once in a while.

We would build a massive fire down where 'base' was to keep warm in between the games. Some nights it could get pretty cold plus it would be pitch black if the moon wasn't out. The fire shed a little light on a dark night.

Later we would cook hot dogs over the fire and make smores. It was always a fun night listening to the stories of where everyone hid.

Most of our church kids lived in town. They didn't get the opportunity to roam the hills on a farm and explore the outdoors. So coming out to that farm was a fun experience for them.

Tandlemuir could be a pretty scary place for big city kids. The wind would howl and rattle through the trees. You would hear strange noises and your imagination would run wild. Most of the time the kids hid in groups. They always felt safer with a friend not too far away. The boys acted tough, but you could tell they would get scared at times. We eventually allowed flashlights because there were too many scared kids. There is nothing like a little light to brighten your path and make you less fearful. I believe there is a lesson in there somewhere.

Psalm 119:105 *"Thy word is a lamp unto my feet, and a light unto my path."*

Tandlemuir Farm
Lochwinnoch Scotland

Muirhouse

The name of the second farmhouse that we lived in was Muirhouse. Most of the farms in that area had their own name. The two farms we lived on were at opposite ends of Muirshiel Country Park which is a massive park in the western part of Scotland. While the first farm, Tandlemuir, was near the entrance of the park, Muirhouse Farm was on the backside of the park and very secluded. I can probably count on one hand the number of people we saw while living there. The only neighbors we had were sheep and cows.

It took us about ten minutes to get to our house once we turned off the main road. We were in the middle of nowhere. Behind the house, there was nothing but hills and a large lake. The view was incredible on top of the hills. The kids loved it at Muirhouse. They would pack a backpack with snacks and take off in the morning with our dog, Sophie, and go hiking most of the day or build forts.

Muirhouse also had a stream that ran just past the house. There were waterfalls and a couple of big pools, one above the house and one below. On a hot summer's day, we would go wading in the pools.

We had the church people out for large bonfires and fireworks. Almost every Sunday we had the young people in our church out for a BBQ and games in between services. It was a great place to live. I was sad when we eventually had to leave that farm.

While shopping one day, we found a picture that looks pretty close to the view we had on Muirhouse Farm. We have it hanging in our living room. It's a reminder of all the great times we had on that farm in Scotland and how God took care of us and provided a place like that for our kids to grow up. Before we moved to Scotland, I could never have envisioned us living at a place like that.

Skye

Muirhouse Farm, unlike Tandlemuir, was always run to the highest standard. All the fences were maintained and everything was almost perfect. The young man who ran the farm really took care of his sheep. He was always checking the sheep's ears and noses. He spent a lot of time with his flock checking on them and making sure they were okay.

Every year at the same time a team of people would come and shear the wool off the sheep which was always fascinating to watch. It was also fun to watch the sheepdogs work every day as they rounded up the sheep. I can still hear the young man yelling instructions to his dog, Skye.

The difference between the two farms and the two shepherds was night and day. It was the compassion the young guy had for his sheep and how he took care of them that made an impression on me. You couldn't help but think of our Good Shepherd and how He takes care of us.

There were times this young shepherd was compassionate, but there were other times when he had to get after the sheep because they were a stubborn bunch. Sometimes we would hear him say, "Go get 'em, Skye." That dog would nip at the back legs of the sheep. She would get the sheep to go where the shepherd wanted them to no matter how stubborn those sheep were.

You can clearly understand why we are compared to sheep in the Bible. Watching that sheepdog reminded me of how stubborn we can be at times always wanting our own way. We need to allow The Good Shepherd to take care of us and be under His care and compassion. Allow Him to guide and direct you to the place He wants you. Don't be stubborn and go in your own direction.

Muirhouse Farm
Kilmacolm Scotland

Sheep on the hillside

Chapter 12
Scottish Weather

Gales

It was the first winter that we lived in Scotland and we had just put the kids to bed. All of a sudden, the wind began to blow really hard. Then in a matter of moments, it sounded like the windows were going to break from the force of the wind. We went upstairs, grabbed the kids out of bed and went down to the main floor of the house.

There are very few houses that have basements in Scotland so we hid in a closet in the kitchen. Denise called a friend across the street and asked her what was taking place. Her friend told her it was the winter gales and they were no big deal. No big deal? We were scared to death and this was no big deal to our neighbor!

We went through many scary nights during the winters in Scotland. The gales were very damaging at times, but as my Scottish daughter-in-law, Laura, says, "Unless the winds are over 70 mph, we don't really worry much."

We had winds over 100 mph at various times. The gales typically came at night so you had to wait until morning to see what the damage was. We normally had trees down and roof tiles missing. These aren't the piddly little roof tiles we have here in the States. These are heavy, massive roof tiles, and when they come off a roof they are 20lbs of flying missiles. One year, the Catholic church across the street lost its roof during the winter gales. Our church fence came down I don't know how many times.

One year, the neighbor's greenhouse lost its glass panes because they blew over the fence and shattered in our brick driveway.

What's interesting is that the houses in Scotland are very different from the houses here in America. Their houses aren't built like they are in the States because they are built to withstand these winter gales. The two farmhouses we lived in had outside walls that were 3 feet thick. There was always that 3-foot area at the windows where you could sit and look out at the countryside because the walls were that thick.

Are you built to withstand the storms of this life? I'm always amazed at how people handle, or don't handle, the storms of life that come their way.

Some people are solid, others not so much.

What kind of faith do you really have?

Matthew 7:24-26 *"Therefore whosoever heareth these sayings of mine, and doeth them, I will liken him unto a wise man, which built his house upon a rock:*
And the rain descended, and the floods came, and the winds blew, and beat upon that house; and it fell not: for it was founded upon a rock.
And every one that heareth these sayings of mine, and doeth them not, shall be likened unto a foolish man, which built his house upon the sand:"

Thunderstorms

One of the things I missed in Scotland were the thunderstorms that we have here in America. We were lucky to get one or maybe two thunderstorms all summer long in Scotland. We had our fair share of rain, but we hardly ever had a thunderstorm. If we did get one, they were typically during the day so you couldn't really see the lightning against a dark evening sky. That was always disappointing. It's funny the things you miss when you live in another country.

I was always fascinated by thunderstorms. I used to sit on the farm porch late at night when I lived in the States and watch the storms all around us. Recently, here in Mansfield, we've had storms every day. In fact, I'm currently sitting through a thunderstorm as I write this.

Being around storms all the time, I learned to know how far away a storm is by how far away the lightning is from me. I was golfing with my buddies one time in Scotland, and we could see lightning off in the distance. My Scottish buddies were all in panic mode getting ready to head to the clubhouse because they thought the storm was close. I laughed as the storm was probably still over Northern Ireland and a long, long way from us in Scotland. But since those men hadn't experienced these kinds of storms very often in their lives, they didn't know these things. I encouraged them not to worry and finish the round of golf. The storm finally came about an hour after we finished.

We face storms all the time in this life whether it be in our personal lives or in our churches. We need to do a couple of things here;

For those of you who are older and have been through storms, you need to help those who are experiencing a storm that they may not be familiar with. An encouraging word or advice might be exactly what a fellow Christian needs at this moment.

Don't be silent at these times.

For those of you who are younger or may not have experienced such storms, seek out advice from someone you know who has been there and done it. I always encouraged the young people who attended our church in Scotland to seek out advice from the older men and women in the church.

We had great business minds in our church along with nurses, builders, engineers, bankers, mechanics... you name it, we had it. I was always disappointed to hear of young people who didn't seek advice and made a mess of things. If they had just sought out advice, they wouldn't have made such terrible mistakes.

Many times our pride gets in the way, and we think we can handle a situation on our own.

Proverbs 11:14 says, "*Where no counsel is, the people fall: but in the multitude of counsellors there is safety.*"

I've always sought out the advice of people who I know went through similar situations that I was either going through or getting ready to go through. There is nothing wrong with seeking out advice from older, wiser men and women.

Thinking you can handle the situation on your own... Well, that's just foolish.

We make unnecessary mistakes all the time because we don't seek out advice, or we don't listen to the advice that was given.

Chapter 13
Sports

Play Ball

Our children always loved to play baseball. Almost every night in the summer we would have a big wiffle ball game in the front yard. Our farmhouse in the States was surrounded by cornfields. So if you hit one in the cornfield… that was a home run. We would be outside playing ball until we couldn't see at night. It was a fun way to end the day.

That didn't change when we got to Scotland. To make our children feel at home, we would go out and play ball at night. There was a big field across the street behind a row of houses which made a perfect place to play ball. Almost every night we would go play baseball just like we did in the States. The only difference was we weren't playing by ourselves on a big farm in the middle of nowhere. We were playing ball in an area that had a lot of houses and a lot of kids.

The neighborhood kids would come out to watch us, but it didn't take long until they wanted to know if they could play. Soon our little family baseball game had 30 kids playing every night. There would be a bunch of them that would knock on our door wondering when we were coming out to play ball.

Baseball was new to most of the Scottish kids. They grew up playing soccer and knew very little about baseball. Cricket is perhaps the closest thing to baseball for them, but the rules are completely different. In fact, after spending twenty years in Scotland I still don't understand the rules of Cricket.

It wasn't long until the Scottish kids were buying their own gloves and bats. We taught them the rules and showed them how to throw and catch a ball. At that time we played with a tennis ball so no one got hurt. If I remember right, I don't think we ever progressed to a real baseball.

All of this got me thinking one night, if I ever start a church somewhere, we could get a bunch of kids in just by playing baseball in a park somewhere. We could eventually invite them to church and then get their parents to come.

And that is exactly how we started three churches in Scotland.

We used baseball in a park to get the kids to come out. We would eventually invite them to the church's youth clubs. We would see them get saved, and then they would start coming to church.

We had a gym in the first church building at Glenburn, and in the winter we would get the kids to come by playing volleyball or basketball. Sports played an important role in the start of all three of our churches.

Who knew how important those little family baseball games

… in the middle of nowhere

… on a farm in Ohio

… surrounded by cornfields

… would become one day.

Golf

One of my favorite weeks, especially living in Scotland, was the week of the British Open, or as they say… The Open. We had the opportunity to go and see The Open many times while living there. Here's a highlight from one of them.

In the final round of The Open, tournament leader Jordan Spieth hit a wild tee shot way right on the 13th hole that hit off the head of a marshal then proceeded to go even further right. The ball came to rest in a position where Jordan could not hit the ball. Now what? He was already assured one penalty shot, and what he would decide next could possibly cost him a major championship.

He used the rules of golf to his advantage and after what seemed like an eternity he hit his next shot off the practice ground towards the green and eventually took a miraculous 5 on the hole. He then unbelievably proceeded to play the next 5 holes in 5 under par to win his first Open Championship.

After the round, they were interviewing the rules official that dealt with the situation on the 13th hole. He said Jordan's knowledge of his options and the rules of golf assured him to make the best possible decision in that critical situation.

Golf has some crazy, even silly, rules, but they are still the rules. Most golfers don't even know the basic rules. I've witnessed golfers not knowing the rules and not knowing their options many times on the golf course. A lack of knowledge about the rules has cost many golfers tournaments or matches.

For about six years I took care of the Junior golfers who played at Troon, a beautiful coastal town on the west side of Scotland.

I set up the competitions, kept all the boys' handicaps, took them to matches...you name it, I did it. At the competitions, we always set aside a time before the boys teed off to go over the rules of golf.

We also provided booklets for new golfers to help them with some of the basic rules of golf. For the most part, all of the boys did their best to learn the rules as quickly as they could. They wanted to learn the rules.

I get worried about Christians who have no desire to know more about the things of God. It's almost like they are saying, 'Thank you for the salvation you provided for me through Christ, but now just leave me alone. Let me do as I please.' They have no desire to learn or know more about God and His word.

Let me tell you, this is not the salvation of the Bible.

This reminds me of Hosea 4:6 where God says, "*My people are destroyed for lack of knowledge...*"

Often when we come to a critical time in our life,

We don't know God's Word well enough to make a proper decision.

We don't know God's principles that could spare us years of heartache.

We just plow through life making poor decisions that will eventually catch up to us. If we knew God's principles and followed them, our lives would be less stressful and without the painful consequences of our ignorance.

What is possibly worse is knowing God's rules and principles then making a conscious decision not to follow them.

Troon

When the Open was played in Scotland, our family always did our best to attend at least one day of the tournament for a family day out. Everyone in our family enjoys golf so it was a fun day.

We attended other events like the Scottish Open which was usually played less than a half-hour away from us. We went to see the ladies' version of the Ryder Cup being played and also watched a lot of the Senior Tour events. It was always neat to be up close to some of the great names of golf.

Back in 2004, the Open was played at Troon which wasn't too far from our house. My parents came over that year, and I made arrangements for my dad and me to be marshals at the tournament. Talk about a blast. We were able to talk to the players, listen to them discuss strategy with their caddies, and help them find their golf balls. You name it we did it.

We were also issued official marshal vests and hats, which I still have to this day. We were on television a couple of times as well. It was a fun couple of days to be a part of such a large event.

One of the strangest events that took place that year was not on the Royal Troon golf course, but on the golf course right next to Royal Troon. They were using the other golf course as a parking lot and someone drove their car right into a bunker. The car was standing straight up!

The bunkers on the links courses are deep and many times they are hidden from view. In fact, at St. Andrews on the 12th hole at the Old Course if you look at the golf hole from the tee and you can't see any of the bunkers.

But when you get to the green of the 12th hole and look back at the tee, there are probably a dozen bunkers or so on the fairway alone and they are scattered everywhere. What looks like a simple and innocent golf hole from the tee isn't so simple and innocent at all.

I often wonder how many times God protects us from events that we don't see and don't even realize they were there. How close were we from that terrible accident or another tragic event?

I look back and think, "If I left a couple of minutes earlier or if I didn't have to run back into the house for something I possibly could have been in that horrible car wreck."

We don't thank our God enough for His daily protection and guidance throughout our day. All those events we don't see, but God graciously guides and protects us through them all.

My dad and I as marshals at the 2004 Open
Royal Troon Golf Club
Troon Scotland

Chapter 14
Scenery and Seasons

Summer

I used to love the summers in Scotland. The sun comes up really early and doesn't set until late. There is about a week during the summer when it never gets completely dark at night. For some reason, every Monday I'd always be up early. I'm not sure if it was just the adrenaline rush from a Sunday filled with church services, but I could always count on being awake around 4:00 a.m., if not before.

I'd usually get up and go play golf. Golfing at 4:00 in the morning is a little different as you can imagine. For starters, the course wasn't ever really crowded at that time in the morning. It was always so peaceful. The only disturbance you would encounter is a deer jumping out in front of you once in a while. The golf course was up high, and you could look down over the city of Glasgow.

While golfing, I would use the time to go over in my head everything that took place on Sunday. What went wrong, what went right, and what we could improve on in the church. It was a great time to reflect on life in general and to evaluate things.

I think it is so valuable to sit back and relax and make time for evaluation. At times we get busy with full schedules, and something is always interrupting our thoughts. These things can cause us to get distracted from real evaluation. It's helpful to set aside a peaceful time without any interruptions and take the time to reflect on life. What could we do better? What needs to change in our life? How can we be more productive? We need to find time to think.

The Highlands

To get up to the Highlands of Scotland on the west side of the country you have to take this windy, narrow road. I'd even call it a dangerous road. Buses take tourists up through there, but I have no idea how two buses could even pass each other going in opposite directions.

The road goes past Loch Lomond and up into the mountains past some of the most beautiful scenery you could ever imagine. I've been on this road numerous times taking visiting family members or guests up to see the Highlands of Scotland.

One of my favorite places to stop is this parking lot area not too far from Glencoe that overlooks a valley. All around you are majestic mountains with snow caps even in the middle of summer. There is a beautiful lake. There are forests of pine trees, and many times you can see all sorts of wildlife.

Every once in a while, I used to escape up there just to get away. It's a great place to think because it is so beautiful and peaceful. We need places like this in our lives. We need a place to get away and think.

We get so caught up in this rat race going 100 mph, and we don't take the proper time to stop. People tell me that they have so much to get done they don't have time to stop. I was like this for many years as well. I almost felt guilty to stop, but after reading a John Maxwell book several years back I realized that I had to stop.

To properly evaluate your life, you need a quiet spot, a place to hide like up in the Highlands of Scotland.

Fall Colors

I'm not sure about you, but I always enjoy the colors of fall. I'm not thrilled with what's coming next... winter... but I enjoy the fall even if it doesn't last long. I love the golden colors and the amazing shades of red. It really is a color fest of sorts. Sometimes you see a tree and just say, "Wow!"

The trees in Scotland changed colors, but not like here in the States. I always missed this time of year when we lived in Scotland. Being out of the country makes you appreciate the colors of fall a little bit more.

We get accustomed to things in our lives, and many times we take them for granted. One of those things is the mercy of God in our lives. We are so undeserving of the things that God bestows on us. Many times we speed through our life and miss out on all the things that God does for us on a daily basis that, in reality, we do not deserve.

Perhaps we need to slow down a little bit and enjoy what God is doing in our lives. Sit down and look at all the wonderful things He does for us. His mercy, His grace, and His loving kindness are all around us to enjoy.

"And shewing mercy unto thousands of them that love me, and keep my commandments." Exodus 20:6

Winter

One April Fool's Day, we got the largest snow we ever had in Scotland during the time we lived there. In the area we lived, typically we would not get much snow in the winter. In fact, some years it didn't snow at all, and if it did snow it melted away by 10:00 or 11:00 in the morning. But if you lived up in the Highlands of Scotland snow was a different story.

One of my favorite pictures of our youngest son, Jared, is when he is teeing off, and there is snow covering the Cairngorm Mountains in the background… in July. We were on vacation at Aviemore, and they had a cold spell. When we woke up the next morning, the mountains were covered with snow, and it was just beautiful.

But we didn't live in the Highlands. We lived in the Central Belt of Scotland, and we rarely saw snow. Although, the one house we lived in was higher in elevation. It could be snowing at our house, and when we looked down to the main road it would be raining.

This was the case one April Fool's Day. I woke up early, looked out the window, and was completely stunned. It had been a really nice March. We certainly weren't expecting snow, but there it was. It was windy, and the snow was drifting everywhere. We couldn't even get out the main door because the snow had drifted up so high.

We managed to get out another door, and the kids went out and played for hours. But it was funny, when I looked down to the main road there was nothing. No snow at all. We ended up with 17 inches of snow that morning, and it stayed on the ground for about 4-5 days.

We lived up a long, private driveway about ten minutes from the main road, and we couldn't get out. We were stuck until the farmer eventually cleared out our long drive…. three days later!

Chapter 15
Our Third Church

Renfrew

We started our third church in an area called Renfrew which was about 15-20 minutes from our first church in Glenburn.

We started meeting in a primary school, but then it became increasingly expensive so we moved to a community centre run by a private group. We were able to use the community centre twice on Sundays and another night of the week to have Awana for the children in the area.

Each time we started a church, God always provided a place for us to meet no matter what town we were in. God always took care of us. Doors opened not only for church services, but also for youth clubs and Awana so we could minister to the children who lived near the church.

The Renfrew church was really a fun group of people to work with. It was mostly young adults that attended, and they were at our house almost every Sunday afternoon. We had cookouts, played games, and had a great time around our table talking and laughing.

We still keep in contact with some of those young families from that church even today. When we go back to Scotland we meet up for meals and get caught up on the latest in their lives.

The Blessing of Being Faithful

We had three men from one of our supporting churches in Monclova, Ohio, come and help us pass out fliers to let people know we were starting a church. On our last day of passing out these fliers, we hit an area of Renfrew that had large apartment complexes. The first floor of these complexes had four apartments. You climbed stairs to hit four more apartments and then more stairs to the third floor and four more apartments. We did this all day. Needless to say, by the end of the day, we were tired and ready to quit. It seemed like all we got done all day was climb stairs.

We got to the last apartment complex, and we just looked at each other. Who was going to climb the stairs all the way to the top? We just stood outside that building, and nobody moved. We joked about skipping the last building, but we couldn't do that. We decided, to cap off the day, that all four of us would climb those stairs together and put a flier in the last four apartments.

Our first service at Renfrew came about a week later, and we had a really good crowd. One of the families that showed up that Sunday was originally from Zimbabwe. They had just moved to Renfrew, and they were looking for a church. I got addresses from all the people who attended that morning, and I visited everyone that week. Lo and behold that family from Zimbabwe lived on the very top floor of that last apartment complex. I couldn't believe it!

That family became one of our key families in the Renfrew church. They were faithful every Sunday, and they were involved in everything we did in the church. They were a tremendous help to us.

Climbing the stairs to the third floor of that last apartment complex ended up being a tremendous blessing from God.

Working Together

The last eight years we spent in Scotland was at the church in Glenburn where everything started for us. We eventually put the third and first church together to form one larger church. It was a lot of fun having that many people in a church. On most Sundays we had between 70-80 people attend the church, and on special Sundays, we would have over 100.

Our Renfrew church was made up mostly of young adults, but we had a good mix of older families as well that helped stabilize everything. The Glenburn church at that time was made up of older families and only had a few young adults, so when the two churches joined together it created a good mix of ages.

One thing I'm very thankful for is that the older people in the church had so much patience with the young adults. Denise and I are in many churches today where the attitude seems to be 'them' and 'us,' and there is a great division between the older people and the young adults.

Our older adults accepted those who were younger with all the mistakes and problems that come with youth. The older members became great teachers and an encouragement to those who were just starting out in life.

It wasn't long until the young adults were doing most of the music on Sundays. They were also sitting on the church boards, helping in children's clubs, and teaching Sunday School. The young adults were heavily involved in the running of the church.

I hear churches say they have no young families. To be honest, I think the biggest problem is the older adults in the church.

Especially the older adults who are not willing to teach the younger ones for fear these young ones may take their job or position in the church.

What happens when you are dead and gone?

Who is going to do your job then?

Someone who isn't trained to do it?

Our churches need to be training grounds for the future. This is a key element that is missing in churches today. Instead of, 'This is my job and you aren't going to take it' …

How about taking a young adult and teaching them what you have learned in the last 30 years.

How about quit being so power-hungry and fearful that you are going to lose your position and be instructors to the future generation.

I'm so thankful for the older generation at Glenburn who were patient and willing to be teachers to the younger generation. They were an incredible group of teachers.

Chapter 16
Helping Those in Need

Quarrier's Village

For about seven years, we lived just outside of this little town called Quarrier's Village. It was a nice town in the middle of nowhere right on the Gryfe River.

For several weeks, while they were repaving our main road, we had to take a detour that took us through the town of Quarrier's Village. As a result, I became curious about the history of the town. I didn't know much about this little village except that at one time it helped a lot of orphaned children.

The town was founded in 1876 by a devout Christian man named William Quarrier. At the age of three, after his father died, William's family moved to Glasgow. He lived in severe poverty as a child until, at the age of 17, he became a shoemaker in a shoe shop. William later became a very successful businessman and owned several shoe shops throughout Glasgow.

Burdened for the orphans that he saw on the streets of Glasgow, William envisioned a town where these orphaned children could learn about the things of God and at the same time learn skills that would help them become productive citizens. His dream became a reality on a parcel of land that became known as Quarrier's Village.

William built large houses for the children. Each house had a 'housefather' and a 'housemother' to manage the affairs of the house.

William also built a beautiful church in the town called Mount Zion Church. The church became known as 'The Children's Cathedral.' The streets in the village have names like Love Avenue, Peace Avenue, and Faith Avenue. William also built a school and other buildings that were necessary for his vision.

Orphaned children were given a home and a spiritual upbringing. With the help of other businessmen, the children were taught skills needed to succeed in life. Many of the children were eventually adopted by families.

You might not be able to do anything to the extent of what William Quarrier did, but each of us can do something to help this generation that is growing up without fathers.

One man can make a difference.

Ezekiel 22:30 *"And I sought for a man among them, that should make up the hedge, and stand in the gap before me for the land, that I should not destroy it: but I found none."*

William Quarrier

Helping Our Communities

The community around our church in Glenburn had a large population of single moms and many were very young. The thing that probably struck me the most was how worn out these moms were. They were trying to raise the children on their own, and trying to take care of the house on their own, and they were exhausted.

These single moms were always so appreciative of the children's clubs our church ran throughout the year. They also came to our church dinners or family night BBQs. We ran community fun days with bouncy castles, face painting, games, and, of course, food. We had men in our church that would help them with projects around the house.

The statistics of children born into single-parent homes are getting higher every year. Our churches have to prepare for this. It is so important that we have men to stand in the gap.

Ezekiel 22:30 says, "*And I sought for a man among them, that should make up the hedge, and stand in the gap before me for the land, that I should not destroy it: but I found none.*"

God was looking for a man to make up the hedge and stand in the gap for the land. God says He will destroy the land if He doesn't find these men. We need to lose our self-righteous attitude and the attitude that says, 'I've already raised my kids.' These aren't the attitudes that God is looking for.

What is the best way for churches to make up the hedge and stand in the gap? How can we help these single moms and their children? What classes can we incorporate to help them with child-rearing or how to handle finances? How can we provide them with a support system? We need to be making a difference in our communities.

Helping Single Moms

In 1971, 8% of the children born in Scotland were born into a single-parent home. That number has increased to 52%, which means that over half of the children in Scotland are growing up in homes without a father. This is not only causing great problems in the homes but great problems in society as well.

I was reading that the number is just over 33% here in America and rising. I'm not sure the average church is prepared for this. If we really want to reach our communities for Christ, we are going to have to make some adjustments.

Our society is telling us that it doesn't matter what the framework of the home looks like, but nothing could be further from the truth. In spite of what our society says, men and women are made differently. A man brings something different into a home than what a woman brings, and a woman brings things into a home that a man can't provide. Together, under the guidelines of God, they provide a stable environment for a child. When this order is thrown into chaos it isn't going to be long before society is thrown into chaos. Now what do we do? How does the church make adjustments to meet this need?

We as churches have to provide support groups for single mothers who are trying to run their homes without help. Many of the women I ran across in Scotland were completely worn out from trying to do everything on their own. We ran children's clubs in the summer called 'Give mum a break' to allow moms the opportunity to get things done around the house or just have a couple hours of rest. I had moms come up to me with tears in their eyes thanking our church for helping them out. What can you do, and what can your church do to meet the needs of the changing community that you are living in?

Helping Little Children

Matthew 19:13-15 *"Then were there brought unto him little children, that he should put his hands on them, and pray: and the disciples rebuked them. But Jesus said, Suffer little children, and forbid them not, to come unto me: for of such is the kingdom of heaven. And he laid his hands on them, and departed thence."*

We need to find ways that we can minister to the lost. We need to ask questions like;

What is the best possible way we as a church can meet the needs of those in our communities?

Who are those that really need help?

Our churches need to do more. We have turned a blind eye to many in our communities because it is going to take time and effort to minister to them, and let's be honest we are too lazy.

We need to consider the children. In Scotland, we had a social worker in our church. I met with her on many occasions, and she told me point blank that those in need get so much government assistance that they shouldn't have any needs at all.

The problem is the money is used poorly. There are very few that know how to follow a budget. Money is spent on alcohol, drugs, and other items that people don't need. As a result, there is not enough money to buy food for the children.

I'm not sure we fully understand the drug problem in the world today. Right now, here in the States, we have companies that are looking to hire people. I've talked to many businessmen who tell me that they desperately need help, but no one can pass a drug test.

The money people are getting from the government is going for their drug habit or other uses instead of paying their bills and providing food for their children. I know this isn't the case in every household, but it is a serious problem.

I was in the homes of many of the children that came to our youth clubs in Scotland, and the lack of food was obvious. Though it cost our church money, and many times I took money out of my own pocket, we always fed the children who came to our youth clubs. I knew full well many weren't getting fed at home.

Let's be honest, a few packs of hot dogs don't cost that much, and while it may not be the most nutritious meal, it is better than nothing at all. Providing fruit and other nutritious foods as snacks isn't that difficult either.

Whether it's through children's clubs, providing meals, or even doing something like William Quarrier did, there are various ways to minister.

Let's just make sure we are doing something.

Chapter 17
Missions

The People God Uses

There are some churches that have supported us for nearly 25 years now. These churches have allowed us to minister to the people of Scotland and today to minister to countless others.

We are grateful for the churches, and for the people inside of those churches, who have sacrificed and have given what they could to support missionaries like ourselves. Many of you are making it possible for us to help others.

Before becoming a missionary in 1996, I often wondered how my financial gift was helping out a missionary if it did at all. Being on the other side of the fence, we treasured every gift. We were so thankful that hard-working people here in America were sacrificially giving to make it possible for us to reach others for Christ. Your gifts, and my gifts, make it possible to further the Gospel.

Just think of how many people God uses in the life of a missionary so that he can reach people in a different country. It begins with hard-working people who sacrificially give to missions in their home churches.

The money is collected by the ushers of the church. Then it is counted and placed in the church's bank account. Next, the church mission's director or the church treasurer writes out the checks to each mission board that is represented by the missionaries they support.

Then there are the mission boards and the people who work in their offices. At the BEMA mission board, we have two ladies, Judy Matheny and Sandie Walden, who have somewhere in the neighborhood of 80 combined years of experience working in that office. None of us could do what we do without these two ladies. None of us.

At BEMA the mail is collected and all the envelopes are opened. The ladies make a record of who sent the money and where the money is going. Each gift is recorded on a computer, then all the funds are gathered and deposited. Next, checks are written or money is wired for each missionary.

These ladies collect money, keep records, send receipts, write out and send checks, wire money, keep track of the missionaries, and write letters on behalf of the missionaries. The list goes on and on, and they do all of this for all of our missionaries. They are incredible servants of God.

When a missionary leads someone to Christ, many people play a role in that person coming to Christ. The process started months ago when a sacrificial gift was put in the offering and when someone took the time to pray for that missionary. That gift went through many hands before it ended up in the missionary's bank account.

All of this makes it possible for a missionary to share the Gospel with someone in a faraway land. It is staggering to think how many people are involved in the process that makes it possible for a missionary to reach others. People from all walks of life and all sorts of backgrounds come together without knowing each other, but each has a part in fulfilling the Great Commission.

God uses countless people so a missionary can reach one person. Fascinating isn't it?

Mission Giving

There are a lot of misconceptions concerning missionaries and their funding. One of the biggest misconceptions is that missionaries receive a set amount of money every month. I've had church members and pastors ask me, "How much support do you get each month?" My answer is always, "I never know." Then, in an angry tone, I normally hear, "How can't you know how much you are receiving each month?" It's because missionaries do not receive a set amount of support each month. It depends on what comes in.

Some churches give every month.

Some churches give every other month.

Some churches give every quarter.

Some churches give once a year.

Some churches might miss a month or two.

There could be a $2000 difference in your totals from one month to another. As a missionary, you have to constantly save money because you have no idea what your support is going to be from month to month. Some churches could be struggling and you wouldn't see support from them for months. Others might have to cut your support in half for a few months until the church gets back on its feet again. I believe on three different occasions we didn't receive money from churches for an extended period of time because the mission's director was embezzling mission money!

This is why I always tell people if you can give a little more to missions this month do so because you figure some churches aren't going to be giving anything or just a fraction of what they normally give.

Chapter 18
Coming Home

The Exact Day

God is busy at work for us and many times we have no idea or clue that He is there working, but He is. When we first came back from Scotland, we stayed in a mission house that was provided by one of our supporting churches in Cincinnati. Another missionary family had just moved out of the house after an extended stay, and the house opened up on the exact day that we needed a place to stay.

The exact day.

While we were in Cincinnati we were able to report back to all of our churches in the Cincinnati area except for one. Instead of three or four-hour trips every Sunday, we had several trips that were just an hour away or even less. We were also able to rest up and get the remainder of the year's schedule filled.

Without making this too long, we eventually had to get out of the house in Cincinnati. What did God do? He provided another mission house for us from a church that I had never heard of before and a pastor I had never met. The exact day that we had to move out of the Cincinnati house God provided us with another house.

The exact day.

God did so much for us that year working out housing alone and on the exact days we needed a place to stay. God is always at work for us. We may not see Him or even realize He is there, but He is.

God Will Make a Way

When we first came back from Scotland, we were living in the outskirts of Cincinnati. One of our supporting churches had a mission house, and we stayed in that house for nearly a month. At the end of that month, we had to move out because another missionary family was going to be moving in. We had no idea where we were going to move next, and we only had a couple of weeks to get everything figured out.

By chance, I got a hold of one of the 'kids' from our youth group in Carrollton. He and his family had moved to a small community not too far from our hometown of Wooster, Ohio. The church they were attending had just remodeled their parsonage, and they were looking for someone to move into it. Go figure that one. After talking to the pastor, this church agreed to let us stay in the house. It was a stunning old house with beautiful wood floors that became our home for nearly nine months.

I had never spoken in this church. I had never met the pastor. But the church family took us in and made us feel at home. It was like we knew these people forever. The pastor and his wife are two of the sweetest people you will ever meet. When we have a week off with no meetings, we like to sneak down to this church and see everyone.

In all of this, I am reminded of how God takes care of us. When we are following the path God has for us He will make a way to provide all of our necessities in life. There are no accidents with God. God can use anyone or any church to help meet the needs of His people. I'm always amazed to see how God orchestrates and brings His plan together. God will make a way, and most likely it will not be the way we figured God would do it. We just need to learn how to trust Him because our God is more than capable of taking care of us.

God's Timing

In 2016, when we came back from Scotland, we began to realize that there was a possibility we wouldn't be returning to Scotland as missionaries. After about 3-4 weeks of meetings, something just wasn't right.

It was the beginning of a devastating year for us. I call it the 'silent year' because we rarely got any direction from God at all. We just got snippets of direction when we seemed to need it and only at the last possible second.

I'd read books that described preachers and missionaries going through periods of life like this, but to actually live through it was a different story. There were many days I prayed for God to give me something... anything... and all I heard was deafening silence. Day after day of silence. I frantically searched for answers, but there were no answers to be found. I read book after book... said prayer after prayer... but nothing.

The great principle I learned from all of this is that we don't need to worry because God will eventually give us answers. It may not be when we want the answers, but the answers will come. After nothing but silence week after week and month after month in a matter of just a couple of days, everything fell into place.

We got a house, a vehicle, and a job opportunity from BEMA, our mission board in Columbus, Ohio, all in God's timing.

If you are going through one of those clueless times in your life just keep trusting God... be patient... and let God finish the puzzle for you. From God's position, He sees everything clearly, and He has everything under control.

Chapter 19
BEMA

Setting Up House Stateside

When my wife and I came back from Scotland, we had nothing here. We had no furniture, nothing for a kitchen, we literally had nothing. So we began going to auctions to pick things up here and there. We were living in Perrysville, Ohio, where the church Perrysville Baptist graciously allowed us to stay in their parsonage for several months. The house had a big garage so we began filling it up with furniture and household items until God opened doors for us as to where we would be living.

At one of those auctions, there was this old clock. Not too many people bid on the clock so I got it pretty cheap. The clock worked fine, but there was just something a little odd about the case. It looked okay, but the design of it was... well, it just didn't look right.

I took the clock to be oiled and looked over by an Amish man, and I asked him about the top of the clock. He looked at it and said, "The clock was too tall so they cut the top off." He told me it was common for people to do that so the clock would fit where they wanted it to. Though the clock case had been altered, it didn't affect how the clock ran or the mechanics of the clock.

We go through a lot here on earth at times. We face cancer, other illnesses, tragedy, death, and uncertainty. What do we have inside of us to get us through those difficult days? We should have enough inside of us to keep on running no matter what comes our way...just like that old clock.

Hidden Gems Antique Store

I faced criticism when I went to Scotland, and when I decided to travel around and represent our mission board, Baptist Evangelical Missionary Association, or BEMA, I was again met with criticism by most of the people that I talked to.

Good pastor friends that I had known for a long time told me that there was no way for Denise and I to support ourselves while traveling around the country raising money for BEMA and missionary projects.

We lost a great chunk of our financial backing when we told our supporting churches what we were planning on doing, and other churches cut off our support because we came off the mission field. It looked like money was going to be a great obstacle in what we were planning to do.

When we finally got settled back into the country, God gave us a house with a large, separate building on the property. The guy who owned the property before us used the building as a jewelry store. So we began to think,

What to do with the building?

What kind of business can we put into this building that will allow us the freedom to leave when I have meetings or missions conferences?

What kind of business will allow me to work on scheduling meetings and talk to missionaries during store hours?

Denise and I eventually decided to open an antique store to help supplement our income.

Now, let me tell you about my precious wife's interest in antiques. When we traveled, I'd like to stop and look at antique stores. My wife… she would sit in the car. When she did go into a store, she would make a comment like, "Why don't they just get a big dumpster and throw this junk in it?"

Her interest was minimal at best!

Five years later, we are having a great time together going to auctions and getting things for our store. Her interest and knowledge of antiques have grown immensely. Her business degree has also come into play many times, and the store has done what it was intended to do which was supplement our income and make it possible for me to do everything I need to do for BEMA and our missionaries.

When we were on that airplane returning to the States from Scotland, if you would have told us that we would be running an antique store in a year's time we would have laughed in your face. We didn't see that one coming at all.

Hidden Gems Antique Store

Representing Our Mission Board

When I started my current position as a BEMA Representative, I wasn't really sure what all of this was going to look like. I had more questions than I had answers.

How am I going to raise money for mission projects?

Am I going to be on the phone raising this money?

Will I have to travel all over the place?

What is actually going to happen here?

To be honest, it was very frustrating because for a long time God didn't answer any of my questions, and it remained this way for a while.

Personally, I like to have the answers to all my questions, and when everything is in place I like to get the job done. But this new job wasn't working out like that. I had major pieces of the puzzle missing, and it was getting frustrating.

After a long time of waiting on God for some answers, I finally got some. BEMA had a large conference for all of their missionaries who were able to come. At that conference, I met a man who for a long time was a BEMA Representative himself, and he asked if he could talk to me.

We sat down for a meal, and he told me that this job wasn't going to be what I thought it was going to be. He said, "God isn't going to have you in a church every weekend representing BEMA. God is going to have you doing some other things as well. Things like helping struggling churches, helping struggling Christians, helping out pastors, and helping missionaries."

He gave me examples of everything God had him do through the years. After that conversation, everything started to make sense. The pieces of the puzzle began to fit together. The picture was complete.

I'm saying all of this to you because many times life doesn't work out how we envision it. What we have in mind that we are going to do may not be what God has intended for us. God may take us down a path that we never saw coming, or a path that we never saw ourselves on.

Yet, it is the path that God wants us on and needs us on.

At some point, it will probably make sense to us... then again, maybe not.

Do your best with the people God has placed in your life at this moment. It might not be what you envisioned, but God has placed these individuals in your life for a reason.

Do your best where God has you.

You are there for a reason.

An Incredible Journey

Earlier this year, Denise and I were coming back from picking things up at an auction. The back of the van was jammed packed full of things, and we had items tucked all around us up front. I think Denise was holding a nail keg, and there were galvanized tubs along with some other items up front with us. It was tight.

We were talking and laughing at what we were doing. When we were standing there at the altar on our wedding day, we never could have imagined that we'd have a van completely stuffed full of antique items some 35 years later. Never in our wildest dreams would we have thought that any of this would be in our future.

We were just talking the other day about the incredible 'ride' that God has taken us on through the years.

We have been to so many different places not only here in the States but in other countries of the world. There have been countless experiences the average person will never have. We have met wonderful people. We lived in Scotland for over half of our married lives.

Denise and I had no clue what was in store for us, but never in a million years did we ever think we would own an antique store to help supplement our income as we travel around speaking and raising money for BEMA and their missionaries.

*And to think that we would have missed all of this
if we weren't sensitive to God's leading.*

God took us on an incredible journey that sometimes we can't even fathom even though we have lived it. God needed us here... God needed us over there. We just went where God was taking us.

We never fought it.

We just went along for the ride.

I sit back and wonder sometimes... what would have happened if we had told God 'no' at some stage.

No, God. We aren't doing that.

No, God. We aren't going in that direction.

No, God. We have a family now.

No, God. We aren't going to Scotland.

No, God. We aren't going to go down that path.

I'm reminded of the old hymn...

Where He leads me I will follow,

Where He leads me I will follow,

Where He leads me I will follow,

I'll go with Him, with Him all the way.

It's been an incredible journey!

Chapter 20
Principles I've Learned

1. God Wants You to Succeed

Proverbs 3:5-6 *"Trust in the LORD with all thine heart; and lean not unto thine own understanding. In all thy ways acknowledge him, and he shall direct thy paths."*

Through our travels, I've talked to a lot of people who told me that they felt they were called to the mission field, but they never went. Many have told me of their doubts and fears. I've heard things like:

"I didn't know how God was going to work everything out."

"I didn't want to quit a good-paying job to pack up my family and move to another country only to find out that it was a mistake."

To be honest, it's scary to pack up your family and live in a country that you know little about. So, I'm going to share some principles I have learned and hung on to during our journey to Scotland.

1. God wants you to succeed.

God wants to see men, women, boys, and girls come to a saving knowledge of Jesus Christ. God wants to see these converts grow in the faith and eventually reproduce themselves in others. God is all for the Great Commission, and He wants you to succeed in fulfilling that Great Commission. God doesn't want to see you fail. The people you will reach for Christ...God had to send His Son to the cross to die for those individuals.

Now, your definition of success and God's definition of success may be different. Your definition might be having a megachurch on the mission field... God's definition might be for you to spend your entire life translating His Word into a people's language with little or no converts so someone else can come behind you and reap the benefit of your labor.

We wrongfully equate numbers with success. 'You're only successful if you have a massive church' is a thinking from when I was growing up in the '70s and '80s, and that mentality is still prevalent today. I'd rather be part of a smaller church that is reaching their community and the world for Christ than a much larger church that is doing little if anything.

A better definition of success is this -

Have we done what God has set us out to accomplish?

You might see what you have done or what you are currently doing as trivial, but God will view it as being highly important because you were faithful in doing what He wanted and needed you to accomplish.

Just make sure you are faithful in doing what God has intended for you to do.

Don't worry about what others say or what others do.

2. You Will Face Opposition

Joshua 1:5 *"There shall not any man be able to stand before thee all the days of thy life: as I was with Moses, so I will be with thee: I will not fail thee, nor forsake thee."*

Principles to hang on to:

1. God wants us to succeed.

2. You will face opposition.

Just because God wants us to succeed doesn't mean that we won't face opposition. For the first six chapters in the book of Joshua, everything is going great for Israel's new leader. Israel's army has been successful in eliminating the enemy out of the Promised Land. They have been victorious in each battle that they faced. Joshua's army is on a roll.

Then comes Chapter 7 and this little town called Ai. This town is so small I'm sure it only had one traffic light. Less than 3,000 men are sent out to defeat it. The remainder of the army stayed back at camp to get a little rest.

Then the unthinkable happens. Israel's army is defeated and comes running back to camp. Joshua is devastated. He didn't foresee a loss. No one did. Yet here they are being defeated by this small little town. The Bible tells us that Joshua rent his clothes and put dust on his head along with the rest of the elders of Israel because a humiliating defeat just took place.

This was a difficult day for Joshua.

The President of Liberty University, Dr. Falwell, used to tell us that if we attempted anything for God then we were to expect opposition, and that is very true.

Much like Joshua and the Israelite army, we were sailing along in Scotland. Things were going well. We had just signed an agreement with the Baptist Union to lease out their vacant church building with the possibility of buying it in the future. A condition of this agreement was that Denise and I had to purchase the church manse or parsonage, which we did. We finally got moved in, and after a long day of work, I went out to sit on the wall in front of the house.

As I sat there, I began to hear chanting. I looked down the hill and a group of about 15-20 people were walking up the hill towards the church. Now this group of people looked like death warmed over. They were in black with their faces made to look like something from the movie *Night of the Living Dead.* They came up the hill, turned down our street, and stopped directly in front of me. They just stood there for a little while and then one of them spoke up and said, "We will get rid of you like we did the last one." Then they turned and continued walking down the street.

For the next 18 years, they would harass me off and on. They were never violent in any way, but they wanted to remind me that they were there praying for our demise. They would send me letters with coins in them and told me that if I touched the coins I would be cursed. Apparently, they put a satanic curse on these coins. I always took the coins and went out and bought an ice cream cone.

You are always going to face opposition, but don't let it get you down. Remember, God wants you to succeed just like He wanted Israel to succeed. Joshua went back up to Ai and completely wiped them out. But lessons had to be learned. You may have to go through a couple of these learning experiences yourself. You may face great opposition, but don't quit. Get back up and fight another day and know that your God is greater than any opposition that you will ever face... even some misguided Satanists from *Night of the Living Dead.*

3. Trust in Your God

Proverbs 3:5-6 *"Trust in the LORD with all thine heart; and lean not unto thine own understanding. In all thy ways acknowledge him, and he shall direct thy paths."*

Principles to hang on to:

1. God wants us to succeed.

2. You will face opposition.

Another valuable lesson I learned is:

3. Trust in your God

God will equip you with everything you need in order to succeed. God knows everything that is going to come your way... you don't. When I look back on our lives in Scotland, I never dreamed we would experience all the different things that we did, yet God knew. God has your life planned out if you follow Him, and if you trust Him.

'If' is the key word here.

Our problem is that we don't trust Him nor do we allow Him to direct our paths. We try to figure out how God is going to do everything, and when we can't see how any of this is possible we back down and don't go the direction God wants us to.

I've had countless people tell me the main reason they didn't go to the mission field, or why they left the mission field, is because they couldn't see how God was going to work things out for them. It isn't your job to figure things out for God. He doesn't need any help from you or me.

God doesn't want us leaning on our own understanding.

He simply wants us to trust Him with all of our heart. We worry and fret over things that are actually God's problems, not ours.

I'm reminded of Matthew 6:31-32 where the Bible tells us, *"Therefore take no thought, saying, What shall we eat? or, What shall we drink? or, Wherewithal shall we be clothed? (For after all these things do the Gentiles seek:) for your heavenly Father knoweth that ye have need of all these things."* Again, God knows what you need.

God knows you have bills that need to be paid.

God knows your car is going to break down tomorrow.

God knows you are going to have a sizable medical bill next year.

God knows you need money to live on the mission field.

God knows you need money for airfare.

God knows you need $200,000 to pay for a church building.

God knows everything that is going to take place. God doesn't need you to worry about these things or for you to try and figure out how He is going to do them… He just needs you to trust Him.

In my twenty years as a missionary, God supplied the need for every single thing that came up. God never let me down once, and He isn't going to let you down either. But you are going to have to trust Him. Most of the time the need was met in a way that was so bizarre I could have sat there a million years and never guessed how God was going to meet that need.

There is a reason that Proverbs 3:5-6 are important verses to me. I've needed to constantly remind myself to just trust in the Lord. Allow God to blaze the path for you and just follow it. Just keep trusting and keep believing. God will make a way.

You just have to trust Him.

4. Take Care of Yourself Spiritually

I've talked to a lot of people who said they were called to the mission field, yet they never ended up going. Their reasons vary from; 'we didn't see how God was going to take care of everything' to 'we didn't want to leave good-paying jobs to find out we made a terrible mistake.'

The truth of the matter is at the moment there is a great void of missionaries. People are still going to the mission field, but not like in the past. The same thing could be said of preachers as well; churches are closing down because they can't find a pastor. It seems like every church I am in for a speaking engagement is searching for a youth pastor. There are fewer and fewer people going into the ministry. It was the same thing we saw in Scotland. While there were people studying for the ministry, there weren't enough to fill the void.

Another factor is that churches are not interested in the ministers that are coming out of our colleges. In a lot of cases, these young men are not well trained, and this has been the situation for a while now.

A lot of this has to do with the level of Christianity in the country. Young people are not being taught in our homes nor in our youth departments. Our youth departments are not training grounds to prepare young adults for life, let alone the ministry. It's good to have fun, but there needs to be biblical instruction, and this obviously isn't taking place.

All of this leads me to lesson number 4 - You have to be responsible for your own spiritual growth and growth in general. If it isn't being taught... you are going to have to learn it on your own. You have to make time for this.

You have to.

Personally, I like to listen more than I like to read. Don't get me wrong, I read books, but I'd rather listen to a message. In fact, I do my best to listen to a message a day.

If you don't have someone to mentor you, you can find someone to mentor you through messages. There are some great preachers out there today that share truth after truth. I go on YouTube, find one of my favorite pastors, and soak everything in. I write down everything that I learn. I stop the video, write down a great principle, and continue on.

I do the same thing with books. There are times when it takes me forever to read a book. Some are filled with such great wisdom that I have to stop and just think on that one point for the rest of the day. There are days I don't even get through a paragraph because I have to stop and take to heart what I read. I have to allow it to teach me and change me.

I've heard people say they read 20 books in a year like it is some contest or something. I always want to respond, "But what did you learn in those 20 books?" How about reading one book and let it completely change you.

The bottom line is to change… to grow as a Christian, and you can do that by being responsible for your own spiritual growth.

5. Be Where God Wants You

We currently have more missionaries coming off the field on a yearly basis than we have missionaries going to the mission field.

Some of the most miserable people that you meet in life can be found in our churches, that's right.... in our churches.

The people that I'm referring to are those who have been called into the ministry, but for whatever reason they just haven't taken that step of faith to actually do it.

Something held them back.

It could have been fear, their family, a lack of faith, or not being willing to surrender everything over to God. It could be anything.

Here's the problem....they know they were called.

They know they should be in the ministry, and they live with the guilt of knowing that God called them, but they didn't go into the ministry like they should have. Guilt is very powerful. It can be crippling, and living an entire life with guilt can make a person miserable.

I meet a lot of people who say they were called to the mission field, but they aren't in the ministry at all. This is happening more and more. I usually say something along the lines of… "Well, why don't you go now?" They kind of laugh off my question and offer up more excuses. But I can see the guilt, discouragement, and regret written all over their faces. They know they aren't where they should be in life.

This brings me to principle number 5 - Be where God wants you.

Don't be where everyone else thinks you should be or even where you think you should be.

Be where God wants you.

You can't undo the past. The past is done, but there is tomorrow. There is the rest of your life. Why be out of God's will for the rest of your life? Perhaps you blew it. Why blow it for the remainder of your life? Why settle for a life outside of God's will?

Why not go into the ministry now?

How about going to the mission field now?

We were at a church early on in raising funds for Scotland. The pastor was older and looked like he had been the pastor of the church his entire life. I asked him how long he had been in the ministry, and he replied, "Not long." I was taken aback by his answer until he told me that he had just graduated from Bible college at the age of 76!

He was one of those in life who was called into the ministry early on, but didn't surrender. He told me that at age 76 he made it right.

It's never too late.

6. Don't Lose Focus

There are a lot of good causes to be a part of. It's hard to decipher at times what we should help with and what we shouldn't help with. What I have learned to do is ask myself this question -

What is the ultimate focus of what I am doing right now?

For me, it was to grow the church I was a part of at the time whether it was Glenburn, Helensburgh, or Renfrew. That was my main focus, and nothing was allowed to interfere with that focus. Even though a cause may be good, we need to think through the process and determine if it could hinder our main focus in any way.

Recently, I was sitting in a board meeting of a mission. Something was proposed that sounded really good and noble. I can't go into all the details, but everything looked good on the outside. The only problem was that in the future it could have caused problems for the main focus of what the organization was trying to accomplish. We had to stop and discuss the fact that even though what was proposed sounded good there was a possibility that it could destroy the main focus of the organization.

I come across opportunities on a weekly basis that I really need to sit down and think about. They are good and noble things. Things that I would love to do, but they could destroy my ultimate goal and what God wants me to do for BEMA and our missionaries.

Can something good and noble hinder what God ultimately wants me to do? The answer is yes. That is why we need to be very careful in our decision-making. We need to think through opportunities that come our way. We need to be cautious. We need to seek out the advice of others. We need to take time to pray about these things.

7. There Will Always Be Critics

We are on our 7th principle to remember as we serve God and seek to do His will in our lives. Here's a quick review of the principles we've discussed so far:

1. God wants us to succeed.

2. We will face opposition.

3. Trust in your God.

4. Take care of yourself spiritually.

5. Be where God wants you.

6. Don't lose focus.

I was reading the other day about Moses. God was in the process of doing something great with the children of Israel. God was bringing His people out of the bondage that they faced in Egypt, and He was taking them to the land of Canaan which He promised to Abraham years earlier.

God called Moses to lead the children of Israel out of Egypt. Moses had a job to do, and he carefully followed the instructions that God had for him. Moses was also responsible for a lot of people, and as is typical, not all of the people were happy campers. As a result, Moses faced criticism from the people and a lot of whining and complaining. The complaining seemed to be nonstop. When you read through the book of Exodus you just want to tell these people to stop complaining.

Some of the people even wanted to go back to Egypt. Think about that for a minute, they wanted to go back to bondage.

That tells you a lot about human nature. Given the choice, there are people who would rather be in bondage than be free. But that is another topic for another day. I want us to concentrate on the fact that Moses was doing exactly what God wanted him to do yet there were still people complaining.

This brings me to lesson number 7 - We can be following God and doing exactly what God wants us to do, and people are going to criticize us and complain.

We can be leading people to something far greater than they have ever experienced in life, and they will complain. Sometimes the complaining can be nonstop.

We need to remember that our responsibility is to follow God, not to be men-pleasers. It doesn't matter what you do, you are not going to please everyone. Our responsibility is to do the job that God asked us to do. God is the one we need to be worrying about because there will always be critics.

Here are some questions I have for us today -

Are we following God or have we allowed other people, through their complaining attitude, to get us off track?

Are we pleasing God or are we trying to please others just so they won't complain to us anymore?

Let's be honest, constant complaining can wear you down.

Stay focused on the job at hand.

8. Guard Your Time

We only have so much time in this life. There will be a day when you take your last breath here on earth and then that is it. There will be no more time.

Time is of great value. I've always been very conscious of my time. I usually have my day pretty well planned out so as not to waste any time. One of my understudies in the ministry said to me, "I can't believe how much you get done in a day." I wasn't always as strict with my time as I am now, but the older I get the more concerned I am with where my time is going and with whom.

A question I have for you today is - who gets your time?

Take a close look at your schedule. Who uses your time? If you don't keep a schedule, start doing so. Write down who you are spending time with. At the end of the week, take a look at what you did that week. We don't realize how much time we waste until we keep track of where our time is going.

I hear people say that they don't have time for this or that, especially when it comes to church. The truth of the matter is that you probably do have the time, but you don't spend your time wisely. You have the time, but you just wasted an hour doing nothing. People waste a lot of time. We can always use our time better. There are days when I feel that I can't put anything else in my schedule, but usually, I can make room.

Can we waste our time trying to help other people? Yes. I had this young man who wanted me to do a Bible study with him. He would show up late and then sometimes not at all. He didn't learn what I was teaching him, nor did he try to learn on his own.

I cleared a space of time for him, and he essentially wasted the time I was giving him. So eventually, I stopped meeting with him.

There are times in your life when you are going to have to make a hard decision about people. Is the time you spend with them beneficial or could you be spending time with someone else who is actually going to learn from the things you are teaching them? I'm confident the old devil brings people into our lives to waste our time. You are going to have to weed those individuals out.

Now, what I'm going to tell you may sound harsh; but, especially if you have children, you will be better off spending time with your children than with someone in your church who will never amount to anything. I look back on my life and remember the preacher's children getting put on the back burner for a disgruntled church member. That is never a good thing.

I remember one Mother's Day in Scotland some church member was having a fit about something in the church. They called and demanded that I come over and listen to their complaints - on Mother's Day!

They really had a fit when I told them no. I was spending Mother's Day with the mother of my children and that was that. These disgruntled, miserable, complaining people eventually left the church, and they are no longer a part of my life.

But I still have the mother of my children.

Remember that, guard your time.

Don't waste it, and don't allow other people to waste your time either.

Epilogue

As I travel from church to church, I often have people come up to me and tell me that they felt earlier in their life they were called to the mission field. Then, with a dejected look, they tell me that they never went. There is usually an excuse given, one they aren't even buying themselves.

There is the fear of the unknown.

There is a lack of control.

Doubts.

Fear.

Anxiety.

Uncertainty.

It's a lot to overcome.

We need to be reminded that we serve the same God that Abraham, Isaac, Moses, Joshua, David, Daniel, Paul, and everyone else in the Bible served. I often think about Abraham. I think about how he packed everything up and left Ur to go to a land he knew nothing of. He just followed the instructions of God.

Around this world, there is a great need for the gospel. We need those who are called to pack their bags and go to a land they know nothing of having full confidence that God is more than able to supply each and every need.

God takes care of everything. Just surrender and go.

I can't believe that God allowed me and my family to go to Scotland. What a great journey. I wouldn't trade it for anything in this world, and our kids will tell you the same. It was an amazing time full of everything that you can imagine.

Of course, not all of our experiences were good, but they got left behind and buried underneath the mountain of great memories that we have.

Scotland changed our lives forever, and I miss it every day.

Just go my friend… just go.

Proverbs 3:5-6 *"Trust in the LORD with all thine heart; and lean not unto thine own understanding. In all thy ways acknowledge him, and he shall direct thy paths."*

Appendix

The Things I Miss About Scotland

Church Sounds

As we travel around from church to church people always ask us, "What do you miss the most about Scotland?" We have so many fond memories of Scotland it's hard to narrow this question down to just a couple of things.

It's the place where our children grew up.

It's the place where we met so many wonderful people in church and out of church.

It's the place that changed our lives forever.

It's the place that made us who we are today.

Our lives would be so different if we hadn't lived there.

But here are some of the things I miss about Scotland.

I miss the singing in the church at Glenburn. When we first moved into the church building, the auditorium had wooden floors and wooden benches so when the people sang the sound just exploded in the auditorium. At that time there were just a handful of people, but it sounded like a choir of 100 people singing in that church, especially when it came to singing the old hymns.

It didn't matter how big the church was when we came back to the States, nothing compared to the singing in the church at Glenburn.

It was a combination of heartfelt appreciation to a God that saved them and the natural acoustics that came with the construction of that building.

Something else I miss is the sound of the baptistry getting filled up. It was a weird setup to fill the baptistry tank with water. We had to run a hose from a faucet in one of the adjoining bathrooms to get water into it. The first time we filled it up was on a Saturday night. On Sunday morning, I went to check the temperature of the water, and the water was gone! The water had completely leaked out. It was going to cost us 1,000 British Pounds to get the leak fixed, which we didn't have. I was so upset about that. We had people to baptize and no way to get the baptistry fixed.

Then one of the ladies in the church provided the money we needed to get it fixed. She told me that she thought we were going to be using the baptistry a lot in the upcoming years. I'll never forget that kind gesture. A lot of people did get baptized in that church including both of our boys and our daughter-in-law, Laura.

I also miss the noise and chatter that took place in the gymnasium during a church dinner. If you know anything about me, you know that we had our share of church dinners. I was usually the last one to get down to the gym after the service, and once I left the auditorium I could hear all the noise. There was something comforting about the sound of all the laughter and banter.

I still miss all of those church sounds.

The Care and Compassion of the People

I will forever remember our church people. We had people from every walk of life. We especially had a lot of church members that were a part of the medical field. I gained a greater respect for everything they did not only at their work but in the church as well.

The nurses in our church would check up on members that had medical problems. They always had a deep concern for others. It was never a fake concern or anything like that, but a genuine 'I want to know how you are doing' concern. They always went out of their way to make sure our church people were taking care of themselves, especially our older members.

When I would visit the older members of our church many times they would tell me that one of the nurses had just been there checking up on them to make sure they were okay. These nurses used the talents and abilities that God gave them to help others at work and to help those in the church. It was a tremendous ministry and one I learned to greatly appreciate.

I always felt their compassion for others was the same compassion that Christ had. That type of compassion had a great impact on our church family. It is vitally important that all of us use the talents and abilities that God gave us to help the church family. These talents have been given to us not only to pay our bills but to help strengthen and encourage others.

The church in Glenburn was a church that had great compassion for others… the saved and lost alike. No matter what came up the church people were always there with a helping hand.

The need could have been financial or it could have been a physical need. It didn't matter, the church people would step up to the challenge.

It also didn't matter if the individual who had the need was part of the church family or someone they never met. That type of compassion isn't in a lot of churches today. That 'family' mentality is missing in our churches.

I miss all the church people who helped out in so many other ways.

Those who helped with the music.

Those who sat on church boards.

Those who helped in the youth clubs.

Those who helped in the kitchen.

Those who were just there for others.

Those who used their talents and abilities to serve.

All of these people gave hours of their time to make our church better. It was a great group of people to work with, and they are deeply missed in our hearts.

The Great Food

One of the first things that we do when we go back to Scotland is get fish and chips. Typically, when a restaurant here in the States has fish and chips on the menu, understand that it is nothing like getting fish and chips in Scotland.

The cod or haddock is always deep-fried to perfection. Then they ask you if you want salt and vinegar? The answer is always, 'Yes.' You have to get salt and vinegar on your fish. Nothing compares to that deep-fried, salt and vinegar-tasting fish.

Then the beverage of choice is always an Irn-Bru. What is Irn-Bru? It's hard to describe. We don't have a carbonated drink that is similar to the taste of Irn-Bru here in the States. It's almost like a cream soda, but not really. The combination of Irn-Bru and fish and chips is… well, no words can describe it. If you ever go to Scotland, ask someone for the best fish shop in the area. Go and enjoy the experience, and don't forget the Irn-Bru.

Besides fish and chips, my favorite food in Scotland was always found at our church dinners. If I could have gotten away with having a church dinner every week I would have. Our church ladies could flat-out cook. Then being an international church not only did we get great Scottish food but we had food from all over the world. We had food from the African countries, Greece, Ireland, and the Philippines. Then there were the desserts. There were some church dinners where I just started with dessert. The ladies of our church always put on first-class dinners, and the food was always excellent.

Haggis anyone? Haggis is a Scottish dish consisting of sheep organs mixed with oatmeal, suet, and a bunch of seasonings.

It is usually cooked in the stomach of an animal, but for the most part it is boiled in a bag made of… well, I'm not sure what the bag is made of. Perhaps it's better that we don't know. If you can get past what haggis actually is… it's really good.

I usually have haggis when we go back to Scotland for a visit. It goes really well with chicken, but I will eat it with just about anything. It is another one of those foods that you need to try if you ever get the opportunity to go to Scotland. Go to a proper restaurant and get some haggis, tatties, and neeps. You'll be glad you did.

Traditional Scottish Fish and Chips
Reproduced with permission by 'The Chaotic Scot'

About the Author

Rev. Barry R. Williams

Rev. Barry R. Williams was born in Wooster, Ohio. At the age of seven, he came to Christ in his home church West Hill Baptist. After graduating from Wooster High School, Barry attended Liberty University in Lynchburg, Virginia. He graduated in 1985 with a degree in Church Ministries with an emphasis in education.

Upon graduating from Liberty University, Barry and his wife, Denise, taught in a Christian school in Wintersville, Ohio. Barry also coached soccer, basketball, baseball, and girl's softball. While attending Wintersville Baptist Temple, Barry started and ran a bus route in neighboring cities.

For the following five years, Barry was the youth pastor at Carrollton Baptist Temple in Carrollton, Ohio, and also taught in the Carroll County Christian Academy. He started a soccer team in the Christian school and coached the basketball team. In the spring, Barry coached baseball at the local high school in Carrollton.

In 1991, Barry took the pastorate at Lodi Baptist Temple in Lodi, Ohio. He pastored the church for five years. It was through the church's extensive missions program that Barry felt the call to missions.

In June of 1996, Barry and Denise surrendered to be missionaries to Scotland. After two years of deputation, they arrived in Paisley, Scotland, where they started Southside Baptist Church which later became Glenburn Baptist Church. In 2001, they were able to help purchase a beautiful building for the church. Barry also started churches in Helensburgh and Renfrew over the following eighteen years.

Barry is now a representative for the mission board BEMA which is located in Columbus, Ohio. He travels the country speaking in churches and Christian schools about missions and the need for missionaries. He also raises funds for the BEMA office and special BEMA missionary projects. His life verses are Proverbs 3:5-6 which have played an important role in his life many times.

Barry and his wife, Denise, have three grown children and four grandchildren. His hobbies include reading and golfing, and he is a lifelong Cleveland sports fan.

For more information, you can contact Rev. Barry Williams at: ECLPublications@outlook.com

About the Author

*The author guiding
on Longs Peak.*

Jack Gorby, a professor of law at The John Marshall Law School in Chicago, acquired his love of mountains and climbing while a student at the Universities at Tuebingen and Heidelberg, Germany, in the early 1960s. His climbing adventures have taken him to the Alps, Mexico, the Andes, the Alaskan Range and all over the lower United States.

For twelve years he was a mountaineering guide for the Colorado Mountain School in Estes Park, Colorado. He met Joe Stettner while doing a slide program at a Chicago Mountaineering Club meeting in the mid-1970s. Over the years, a warm and close friendship developed, during which time Joe regaled Jack with the stories that comprise this book. Jack is a member, and former president, of the Chicago Mountaineering Club and a member of the American Mountain Guides Association, the American Alpine Club and the Colorado Mountain Club.

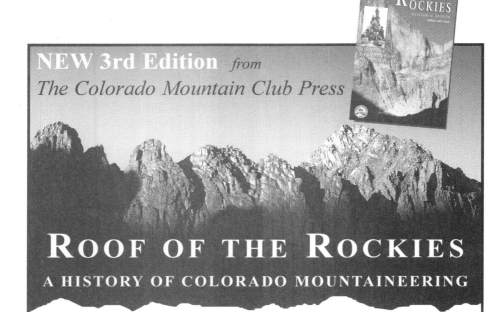